The Phan

The Great Lakes ore carrier [illegible] in eastern Lake Superior on November 10, 1975, during a bad storm. All hands were lost. Its remains were not positively identified until May 21, 1976. But on Halloween night, October 31, 1980, my boyfriend Jerome Renner and I saw the Fitz.

The city of Duluth is built on the hills around the west end of Lake Superior and a scenic route at the top of the hills runs the length of the city. That Halloween night my boyfriend drove along Skyline Drive and stopped for a panoramic view of the city.

In the harbor we saw a stationary ore boat. It was not parallel to the docks as boats usually are but at a funny angle. All American boats show a specific individual light pattern at night and none is duplicated, especially after a sinking. We recognized the carrier as the Edmund Fitzgerald.

For such a large ore carrier to enter the harbor, the Aerial Bridge has to go up. Jerry later talked with the men on the bridge. They told him they saw the boat coming, signaling to raise the bridge. They acknowledged and raised it. They told Jerry they could hear the sounds of sledgehammers opening the hatches as the boat passed under.

The phantom ship was gone without a trace the next day.

—Wendy Mitchell, Duluth, Minnesota
February 1988

Other books in the
"From the Files of FATE" series:

From Flying Toads to Frogs with Wings
Dr. Karl P. N. Shuker

Mysteries of the Deep
compiled and edited by Frank Spaeth

Out of Time and Place
compiled and edited by Terry O'Neill

Phantom Army of the Civil War and Other Southern Ghost Stories
compiled and edited by Frank Spaeth

Psychic Pets and Spirit Animals
compiled by the Editors of FATE

Strange but True
compiled and edited by
Corrine Kenner and Craig Miller

True Mystic Experiences

Fascinating Real Life Stories of Spirits, Other Dimensions, and Strange Phenomena

From the Files of FATE Magazine

Compiled and Edited by
Jennifer Spees

2001
Llewellyn Publications
St. Paul, Minnesota 55164-0383 U.S.A.

FIRST EDITION
First Printing, 2001

Book design, layout, and editing: Jennifer Spees
Cover design: Lisa Novak

Library of Congress Cataloging-in-Publication Data
True Mystic Experiences: fascinating real life stories of spirits, other dimensions, & strange phenomena: from the files of *FATE Magazine* / compiled and edited by Jennifer Spees. —1st ed.
p. cm.
ISBN 1-56718-262-3
1. Parapsychology — Case studies. 2. Spiritualism—Case studies. I. Spees, Jennifer 1976– . II. FATE (Chicago, Ill.)
BF1031 .T78 2001
133.8—dc21

00-050646

Llewellyn Worldwide does not participate in, endorse, or have any authority or responsibility concerning private business transactions between our authors and the public.

All mail addressed to the author is forwarded but the publisher cannot, unless specifically instructed by the author, give out an address or phone number.

Llewellyn Publications
A Division of Llewellyn Worldwide, Ltd.

P.O. Box 64383, Dept. 1-56718-262-3
St. Paul MN 55164-0383

Printed in the United States of America

Contents

Amazing Animals 39

Family Ties 73

Introduction

A woman dreams of her son's fatal car accident seven years before it happens. A mother's spirit returns to leave a final written message for her daughter. Two men out deer hunting on a cold, snowy November day discover a warm, sunny spring meadow but are unable to find it ever again. For over 50 years, the readers of *FATE Magazine* have submitted their true stories of strange, unexplained, and paranormal experiences.

True Mystic Experiences has been one of *FATE's* most popular features since 1948. These are firsthand accounts of extraordinary events happening to ordinary people. Each author has submitted a signed and notarized statement swearing to the truth of their experience.

Skeptics may insist that many of these stories can be attributed to sheer coincidence, hallucinations, dreams, or any number of so-called 'logical' explanations. Perhaps the skeptics have a point. But the most important thing is that each person felt that their experience was significant, and, in some cases, lifesaving.

As you read these stories, one constant theme emerges—there are more things in this world than we normally perceive, or perhaps even understand. I hope you enjoy reading these stories as much as I have.

Guardian Angels

Some people may refer to their guardian angel as God, a spirit guide, a totem animal, or an ancestor. An angel may appear as a living, breathing human being to help a traveler in need. Others may hear a disembodied voice shout out a lifesaving warning. Those who have had such experiences believe that we do not go through life alone.

The Religious Medal

This adventure started the day I received the letter from my parents enclosing a promised religious medal. Being in the Army, away from home, I had vowed to continue my church teachings and had asked my parents to send a special medal that the church was making for the men in service.

I placed the medal on my key chain to carry with me at all times. The loop of the medal was small but after several minutes of careful manipulation I got it on.

Two weeks later, upon returning from a night problem, I decided to change my dirty fatigues as we were going to fire the .50-caliber machine gun early the next morning. I was transferring the key chain to the clean uniform when I noticed the medal was off the chain. "Oh well," I thought, "the key chain has broken before." But upon examining the chain I saw that it was still intact. And to my surprise, the loop of the medal was not broken either. How could it have come off when the key chain was not open?

Too tired to figure it out, I opened the chain in order to replace the church medal. The medal wouldn't fit. I asked one of my buddies to try it but he, too, had to give it up. It wasn't until another one of my friends swore that the medal could not possibly go on the chain that I placed it in my billfold and fell into bed.

The next day began as usual. We prepared to fire the .50-caliber machine gun.

I don't recall exactly what happened. There was a big explosion and the next moment everything went black.

The machine gun had blown up while firing.

Later, after assuring the officers that I was all right, I continued a careful search of my body as there were splinters of steel everywhere. I took my wallet from my breast pocket. Imbedded in the wallet was a one inch sliver of steel. I pulled it out of the leather and saw that the point was blunted—blunted by my church medal.

Except for the medal the splinter would have entered my heart.

I still wonder what beneficient force removed the medal from the key chain and kept me from replacing it.

—Sgt. James L. Cole, Fort Sill, Oklahoma
February–March 1952

Who Were They?

A friend and I were driving home from a party late one Saturday night in January 1940. We were proceeding down the narrow pass at Castellemore, Malibu, Pacific Palisades, when I asked him to park for a few minutes because I wanted to get out. He wheeled up to the shoulder of the road and asked me to hurry because it was late.

I put my hand on the door handle and looked up in surprise because there, in that lonely spot, a man and a woman loomed up beside the car door, very friendly and chatty, but apparently determined to linger and deter me. I gave up getting out of the car and let them talk. They seemed to know me very well and were full of jolly anecdotes and laughed a great deal.

My friend finally roused himself and said, "Who are you talking to?"

I looked around and they were gone. Then Casey got out of the driver's seat and went around to the rear of the car. In a moment he got back in, very sober-faced and pale. He backed the car out slowly and carefully and then parked it again. He wiped his face on his handkerchief.

"If they hadn't stopped you, you would have stepped out into space," he said. "It is a drop of about 1,000 feet."

He asked again who the people were and where they went. I told him they just disappeared and he said, "They had no place to stand. They could not stand in the empty air, could they?"

Whether they could or not, they did. They held the car door and talked until Casey got out, and they refused to move away until then.

I had never seen either of them, and did not know them, but they seemed like ordinary people in ordinary clothes.

—Miss Eva Roe, Los Angeles, California
July 1950

An Angel on Our Doorstep

God speaks to us in many ways, but how often do we listen? We should have been warned, or at least a little cognizant, when the pain occurred.

My husband John and I arrived home at noon on that Monday, having spent a stressful but fun-filled weekend with our daughter and her family. We were running late, so we were scrambling to get the car unloaded and go golfing when we were interrupted by the ringing of the doorbell.

Standing at the door were two women. The one who appeared to be in charge introduced herself, explaining that she was taking a survey of the 1993 flood and the effects it had on the neighborhood and our household—which, incidentally, experienced no flooding.

I asked them both in, but only one entered. I explained that we had not had any trauma or hardships at all in connection with the flood. Then the woman said she was also taking blood pressure readings, and asked if I would like mine taken. I explained that we were short of time, but consented to having my blood pressure taken.

My husband walked through carrying the TV. "What are you doing, Kay? We're in a hurry," he said.

"You should be taking HIS pressure," I insisted to the nurse.

"No way!" was his emphatic reply. "We haven't the time."

Reluctantly, however, he sat down and the cuff was put in place. Reading her instrument, the woman told John: "You should go to the hospital now!" John replied that we did not have the time.

"Well, if you were my husband we would be on our way right now." And with that the woman left. I looked out later, but I could not see her outside.

A quick phone call to the nurse at work gave John the same advice: Go to the hospital! In spite of this, we continued on our way to the golf course.

Two significant chest pains later we were on our way to St. Luke's. At the hospital, it was swiftly determined that John was having a heart attack.

Two days later, John was recovering from a quadruple bypass. Miraculously, all four of our children made it home in time for the surgery. The doctor told us that had we gone golfing that Monday, John would have had a massive heart attack.

I checked with my neighbors later, and found that no one else had ever been contacted by anyone concerning the "flood of 1993," nor did anyone even see the women at our door. So who was that woman—Johnny's Guardian Angel? I think she was.

—Kay Woodhouse, Delhi, Iowa
February 2000

Near-Fatal Water Lily

Do you believe in guardian angels? I do and I'll tell you why.

When I was a little girl, about 55 years ago, three blocks from where we lived there was a slough of quicksand. Anything unfortunate enough to wander into it was sucked down into a watery grave. This slough had a thick green scum covering it and just a few weeks after my own experience a neighbor's cow mistook that lush-looking green for the real thing and went down and never came up again. Many were the admonitions I heard to stay away from that evil spot!

One Sunday afternoon, being a little early for Sunday School, I wandered past the slough to a friend's house, but as she wasn't ready to go yet I decided to go back home alone. On the way back I spied the whitest, most beautiful water lily imaginable.

Forgotten were all the warnings and admonitions I had ever heard.

The water lily seemed to grow very close to the edge of the slough, so close that I would have no trouble at all reaching it—or so I thought. But, when

I reached for it, it was farther away than I expected and I went in and down, down, down—until I was in the water up to my shoulders. Vaguely I wondered what would happen when the water reached my mouth.

Then the sweetest music began ringing in my ears. And it happened! A strong hand grasped the back of my dress and I was slung, literally slung onto the dusty road 10 feet away from the slough.

Unhurt but badly shaken, I still had the curiosity to look around to see who had rescued me. There wasn't a soul in sight, not an animal, and not a sound to mar the Sabbath stillness.

—Louise Mathae, Lewistown, Montana
July 1960

We Are Not Alone

In 1928 I spent several weeks at a summer resort in the Colorado Rockies. It was a beautiful spot surrounded by pine forests, lakes, and mountain streams. I especially enjoyed walking at night among the fragrant evergreens with the pale moonlight filtering down through the branches.

One night, with the moon full and the air sparkling, I left the trail and strayed into a deeper part of the forest. When I grew tired I looked for the trail only to discover that I was lost. I kept searching for the trail but seemed to be getting into deeper woods.

Finally I came upon a small clearing and some yards ahead I saw a tumbledown mountain cabin. As I approached it an overwhelming sense of foreboding like a cold, clammy hand stopped me dead in my tracks. At that moment the moon went behind a cloud and in the darkness I stood gripped by a fear of impending evil and violence. Cold perspiration broke out on my forehead. I started forward again but once more an invisible hand seemed to stop me.

Then about 10 feet ahead of me a soft glow appeared. Astonished, I saw that the light formed the outline of a tall robed figure, the details of which were not visible. The figure pointed off into the forest to my right.

All fear left me and a warm feeling of peace possessed me. Almost as though a voice were speaking, words echoed on my inner ear, "Have no fear for you are not alone!" Then the figure vanished.

I walked swiftly in the direction the figure had indicated. In a short time I came upon the trail and was soon safely back at the hotel.

The following morning the alarm was spread that a violently insane murderer had escaped the previous day and was believed to be somewhere in the woods. He was captured late that day in the tumbledown cabin where he had been hiding the night before when I was in the woods.

—Paul M. Vest, Santa Monica, California
February 1954

Early Morning Tea

My wife Dorothy and I are now retired and living in Blue Springs, Missouri, in a minister's retirement home. During World War II, however, I was a social worker in South Chicago, Illinois.

We lived in an old building that had been condemned in 1935. In the spring of 1945 I awoke one morning and had a strong desire for a cup of hot tea. I carefully got out of bed so I would not wake my wife, but when I opened the kitchen door beside the bed, there she was, sitting in the dark, enjoying a cup of hot tea. Early morning tea was not customary with us.

We didn't even have time to wonder why we had both been given a strong urge to have a cup of hot tea before there was a tremendous roar from the bedroom. When we opened the door we were amazed to find that the entire ceiling of the bedroom, about seven feet by seven feet, had collapsed! Lying on each of our pillows, edgewise, was a big piece of plaster, one inch thick and over two feet square. Had we been sleeping, our heads would have been crushed by the plaster.

Our guardian angels, or whatever you wish to call them, had awakened each of us and instilled an urge for hot tea or we both would have exited this world in 1945. Obviously we had much more work to do. We're still around after a long career in the ministry.

Dorothy Poppe, R.N., has also been a geriatrics and nursing home specialist.

—Louis and Dorothy Poppe, Blue Springs, Missouri
February 1992

Timely Warning

On a Saturday in February 1970, I moved into a downstairs apartment near the Sacramento High School in Sacramento, California. It was a neat building in a well-kept neighborhood and I felt completely safe.

However at 3 A.M. the following Saturday I was awakened by the sound of breaking glass. Then a voice spoke to me from a corner of the room, "You are going to be murdered tonight."

I didn't question whose voice it was or where it came from. I was immediately filled with dread, and I rose, dressed, and waited for morning to go out and find another apartment. I had moved into the new apartment by 2 P.M. when I was suddenly taken by a violent chill.

The following Saturday I went back to the original apartment to finish settling my bill. The manager looked at me strangely and then said, "It's a good thing you moved out when you did. That night, someone broke into your apartment and completely wrecked the place."

Later, I asked the psychic Betty Bethards of Novato, California if that was my guide who warned me and she said very positively, "You better believe it!"

—Merla Manor, St. Petersburg, Florida
October 1993

Angels of God

It was a cool evening with the threat of rain when Jack and I got into his truck to go to Monicello, Mississippi for a football game. Torrential rains caused the roads to be slippery and nearly blinded us. The night had a swarthy, hostile look.

After driving more than halfway there, we decided to turn back. Listening to the constant downpour and the windshield wipers, I became sleepy and laid my head on Jack's shoulder. After a few minutes, I heard Jack mumble something about the roads being too slippery. When I opened my eyes I could see one dim headlight coming from the opposite direction, headed straight for our truck.

The next thing I knew, I was floating high in the air among the now visible stars. As I hovered over the ground, I saw myself in the back seat of a car with my head slumped to one side and a bright light surrounding the inside of the car. How could I be in two different places at one time? The warm and secure feeling kept me suspended above earth.

Suddenly, I felt piercing pain and opened my eyes, realizing I was in the back seat of an automobile—not Jack's truck. There was a bright light flooding the interior of the car. A blonde, middle-aged man was driving the vehicle and a blonde woman passenger the same age sat in the front seat.

"Oh my head hurts so much, it feels like it's falling off my shoulders. Help me, please," I cried.

The blonde lady turned around, placed her arm on the top of the front seat, and said, "We are both angels of God and we are here to help you. You are going to be all right. Go back to sleep." I closed my eyes and didn't remember another thing until a week later.

When I woke up I vomited and vaguely remember shapes and outlines of people in my hospital room. A few days later I woke again and Jack was by my bedside. He told me what had happened and that his new truck had been destroyed. No one in the other auto had sustained injuries.

I had been thrown out of the truck, face down into a dirty ditch filled with rainwater and experienced multiple injuries. After careful consideration, I decided the angelic beings were a hallucination.

One evening while Jack was visiting, I asked him who brought us to the hospital, since we were out in the middle of nowhere and there weren't any houses around for miles. He calmly and accurately quoted verbatim the conversation I overheard, adding that he failed to get their names. After dropping us off at the emergency room the Good Samaritans continued on their journey.

I often think about the reality of the event. Occasionally I mention it to others, especially spiritually-minded people, perhaps looking for a mystical answer. After painstaking examination, often with this particular objective in mind, my range of spiritual knowledge has given me a clear concept of truth and enlightenment for the word of God. Recently I was ordained as a missionary and believe this will give me an opportunity to assist others with similar occurrences.

—Jane Maddux, Jackson, Mississippi
May 1993

A Baby Cried

In the winter of 1972–73 my wife and I were renting a lakeside home in northern Minnesota. The bedrooms upstairs were unfinished so Peggy and I converted the double couch in the living room into a bed. Our two-year-old daughter Da'Nel Eve slept in her crib in an adjoining room between the living room and the stairway.

On January 12, 1973, we went to bed at 10 P.M. About midnight I was awakened by the crying of a baby. At first I just assumed it was our daughter but then I suddenly remembered—our little girl was staying with her grandparents. I jumped out of bed and hurried into her room.

That's when I noticed the faint smell of smoke. Dashing up the stairs I found smoke coming out of one of the closets. We were heating the home with a woodstove and the chimney had caught fire.

My wife and I made it out in time and in fact, we saved most of the house. But I shudder to think what might have happened if the mysterious baby had not cried in the night. There is no doubt that it was a warning, but from whom? I guess we'll never know.

—Tom R. Kovach, Akeley, Minnesota
February 1976

Fate's Heavy Hand

I was 12 years old in the late summer of 1939, still young enough to find the stack yards behind my father's stables a delightful place to play. In the evenings while my father spread bedding straw for the animals I wandered between the haystacks. They were high and close together—often not more than three feet apart—and my imagination turned them into strange castles linked by mysterious tunnels. The smells, the soft sounds from the stable, the sweet evening air made this the most enchanting part of my father's Centerfield, Utah, farm.

One particular night after the fall crops were in I played my usual game among the stacks while I waited for Father. I stopped for a moment at the end of one stack directly back of the stable and suddenly I felt a physical blow to my back, as if a strong hand had struck me from behind. I was knocked to the ground where I lay for a moment stunned.

Looking up I saw a pitchfork quivering in the very spot where I had been standing! My father, having finished scattering the straw, had catapulted the fork over the stable, unaware that I was playing behind it.

I do not like to contemplate what might have been my fate if some mysterious blessed force had not pushed me to the ground.

—J. A. Christensen, Salt Lake City, Utah
May 1969

The Hand of God

My husband Tom and I were stationed in Alaska in 1961 and although he was on temporary duty in the Aleutians the children and I were living in a house in Eagle River near Anchorage. There were two routes by which our house could be reached. The long way was about two miles up a gradual hill and the short way was down a flat road and up a steep hill to our street. My friend Anne Ratliff was also alone with her children, her husband being with mine. Her trailer was two miles away or one mile, depending on which route was used.

When I received word that the men might be coming home sooner than the 120 days they were supposed to be away, I wanted to visit Anne. I decided to take the short way and piled my five children into our station wagon and started down "Deadman's Hill," which in January was packed with snow and ice. This road joined the main highway at the foot of the hill at a point just above a bridge over a gorge and a partly frozen river. When I touched the brakes to slow the wagon, they did not hold. In no time my speed had increased to 70 miles per hour. I turned into the skid but nothing worked. The wagon was spinning, gaining speed, and heading inevitably for that highway, that bridge, and that drop. I told the children to lie on the floor and I remained as frozen as the ice outside, holding the useless steering wheel.

I screamed, "Oh God, stop this!"

Suddenly I felt a crunch and the wagon stopped dead on the lawn of a little church. I thought I had hit a church sign but I didn't wait to see. I drove the rest of the way to Anne's trailer.

The children were all right but I had pulled a muscle in my shoulder. I called the police because I thought I would have to pay for the sign I had damaged. They came and looked over the area where I had stopped. I had not hit a sign or a rock buried in the snow or anything else that the officers could see. They didn't understand what had stopped the vehicle. Next they examined my station wagon. The bracing between the door on the driver's side had been pushed and three long thin dents marked the front door on the driver's side. One of the police officers said to me, "That looks for all the world like a partial handprint, a very large one."

I believe God heard me ask for help and He gave it. He stopped the station wagon in the only way my mortal mind can grasp. He put out His hand.

—Joan W. DiNatale, Mesa, Arizona
October 1982

Hand on My Head

The first of seven times I cheated death was during the war-to-end-all-wars. On July 14, 1918, Bastille Day, at 12:10 A.M., we of the Rainbow Light Field Artillery were in sacrifice position near Chalon-Sur-Marne off the Suippes Road, in an abandoned trench system. We were to hold down the German attack. We knew the attack was due through the daring and heroic efforts of several French officers and one private who had penetrated deep inside German lines and fought their way back with storm troopers as prisoners. These prisoners broke and gave valuable information.

As corporal in the horse section of Light Artillery it was my duty to bring up ammunition. At 11:30 P.M. it was found we did not have sufficient harnesses to go get 10 caissons full of shells.

Really it is not more difficult to buy mink coats at Woolworth's with Confederate ten-dollar bills than to convince the guard at an ammo dump (when you find one) that you are who you are and Colonel So-and-So said, "Get shells."

But we got a load—10 caissons—then we got lost and somewhere in the dark we passed the German infantry moving up. We whispered "Wie gehts" and swallowed hard. To the many answers to our greetings we kept still, turned around, and at 3:45 P.M. pulled into the revetment. By this time tempers were short and those fortunate not to have drawn this detail were tucked in their foxholes. We had no holes and the German artillery fire was searching every gully, road, and inch of ground that four years of fighting along this same line had taught them existed.

My assistant stumbled over some baled hay and sacks of oats left by the supply regiment for our horses. We piled this up as a barricade and lay down behind it. At least it provided some shelter from a direct hit. The fear was draining out of our throats somewhat by this time and we decided we could grab a few moments of precious sleep.

I took off my pistol belt which was loaded with two canteens, one extra in case, a first aid box, cartridges, and a musette bag. All this just did not allow one to assume a prone position. As I bent forward to put the heavy belt on the baled hay I felt a hand on my head. This hand pushed me down so hard the rim of my helmet went more than an inch into the hard chalk soil. And at that exact moment a shell tore through my service belt, cut the handle of my .45, took one canteen away with it, and exploded a few yards behind us.

If that hand, or force, or you name it, had not pushed me very forcibly down, my head would have been completely severed from my body.

When I got my heart back down out of my mouth and could talk I turned to thank my assistant. To my surprise he was not there. He told me later he had gone to tie up a loose horse and then couldn't bear to come back for he had seen the shell explode and he was sure I was dead.

—Chester E. Hall, Los Angeles, California
May 1960

The Voice Only Mother Heard

I'll never forget the incident that occurred in late August 1968 when I was 13 years old. Our family group—my mother, my stepfather David Long, my younger sisters Monica and Teresa and I—were returning from a happy vacation in Florida. A few miles south of Chattanooga, Tennessee, my stepfather pulled off the road. He was hot and tired after a long drive and asked Mother to take the wheel. Evening was coming as she agreed to drive and it was already dark by the time we passed through Chattanooga.

As the night wore on we found ourselves about an hour's drive north of Chattanooga. The two-lane road seemed to grow progressively bumpier and narrower as we traveled north. My stepfather had fallen asleep in the front seat. In the rear my two sisters also were asleep and I was on the verge of dozing off.

We had come to a lonely stretch in the road where there were no lights on either side. The road mounted a rise and just beyond this, we learned later, a highway crossed our road. There was no stop sign or signal of any sort to indicate the highway just ahead. Mother was cruising at nearly 80 miles an hour down the deserted road when she reached the rise.

Just as we came to the highway Mother hit the brakes. The car skidded sideways, throwing everyone around. At that same moment a huge tractor trailer rig passed within inches of us, flying down the highway we were about to cross. If the car hadn't skidded sideways the truck would have demolished our Mustang. No one would have survived.

We were all shaken up by what had occurred. My stepfather, awakened by the jolt, stared at Mother in disbelief. "Why in the name of God did you stop like that?" he insisted.

"I wouldn't have if you hadn't shouted for me to stop and shoved my foot off the gas and onto the brake," she replied in a rasping voice.

"But I didn't," he protested. "Maybe one of the kids?"

"No," I supplied. "We were all asleep or almost."

"Maybe you did see a sign," my stepfather reasoned. "It probably didn't register in your mind."

We backed the car and checked around. But there was no sign. So we continued on our way, shaken by our near-miss. To this day we are puzzled by the voice that only Mother heard and the push she felt, but thankful that they saved our lives.

—Laura J. Underwood, Knoxville, Tennessee
January 1975

Interrupted Journey

On July 24, 1996, I was admitted to St. Joe's Hospital for the removal of my left kidney and a rare, massive tumor that was attached to it. The doctor had warned me to settle my affairs before the surgery. I was scared stiff!

I called my best friend Debbie and told her that the doctor thought that the tumor had become attached to my adrenal gland and possibly to my spleen. We talked for nearly two hours and I felt better just sharing my problems with her.

The night before I was admitted to the hospital, Debbie called me. I again said how scared I was. Debbie replied, "Don't be afraid, for you won't be alone. The angels will watch over you, just have faith!"

I went to surgery at seven o'clock, and was in the operating room for four hours. Soon, I was walking down a long gravel path with trees forming a canopy overhead. The trees on both sides of the path kept me from seeing the sky above, but I could see the clear blue sky in the distance. Then I noticed that someone was walking beside me, holding my right hand in theirs. I would feel a gentle pressure or squeeze on my hand from time to time but every time I tried to turn my head to see or speak to the person, I couldn't turn my head to the right. I had no trouble turning my head to the left.

We continued our stroll. As we got near the end of the path, I could see the sky, a brilliant blue. As I tried once more to turn to my companion, I felt a strong reassuring caress or pressure on my hand and I knew that I was not alone. I sat down in the lush green grass to wait for what was to come!

Several hours went by while I was in recovery, and I didn't know that I had nearly died on the operating table until weeks later. The tumor was rare—only one in several thousand are found to be noncancerous. It was only a half inch from attaching itself to my heart.

Debbie called me while I was in the hospital, but I never told her about what had happened to me (my walk to Heaven?) until much later, when I went home. When I had finished telling her my story, Debbie said, "Bette, you weren't meant to see him, that was Joshua, my guardian angel, and he returned to me and told me the crisis was past and you would be fine! I was worried but I knew he would take care of you, even as your guardian angel hovered there with him."

I will never forget the beautiful trees and that long gravel path that I walked with my angels beside me. I knew that God had more in store for me than I could ever comprehend!

Since this experience, I now know why God spared my life. My husband suffered a hemorrhage and died at my feet. I was alone with him when this happened. He passed over just a year and nine months ago. Now I feel his presence watching over me!

—Bette Atkinson-Gibble, Denver, Pennsylvania
March 2000

Camper

My husband Bill, Punks, our half-coyote dog, and I went camping in our pop-up camper on July 4th weekend, 1994, on the Eel River near Peru, Indiana. We had gone to play bingo at the American Indian bingo hall in Peru. Fortunately we were lucky and came out ahead. After we returned to our camper, I went to bed at about 11:30 P.M. I had been coughing and hacking since getting wet the week before, and I didn't feel good. Bill and Punks stayed outside by the river for about an hour and then came inside.

Bill undressed and lay down on his bunk at the opposite end of the camper, petting Punks. It was quiet. Outside the pop-up, to my right, I heard an animal noise that sounded like a cross between a moan and a groan, and which was vaguely familiar. The animal moved down to the area near my feet and the noise grew louder. I wondered why Punks didn't bark or Bill didn't wake up.

The noise changed, grew louder, and started coming from the area outside the camper just above my head, really scaring me. Bill told me to sit up and I did. Instantly the animal was at my feet again, making that noise. I knew that it was going to rip into the canvas and attack me. I swung my feet into the center of the camper and sat facing Bill. He stood up, grabbed a flashlight, and prepared to go outside to confront it. Punks jumped down from the bunk and stood in the middle of the pop-up watching Bill.

Outside the camper, a series of firecracker-like sounds ricocheted to the right and overhead. Within seconds Bill's bunk was hit by a 12-inch diameter tree limb that crashed through the plastic-treated top. Canvas ripped from brackets, and metal supports ripped loose and bent from the mountings. Some were bent into an "S."

If I had not been frightened and warned by the moaning and noises of the animal, Bill would have been skewered through the ribs by the tree limb and Punks would have been crushed to death.

After the people at the campground helped get the tree limbs and debris off our camper, I sat down and concentrated on what had happened. I remembered hearing that noise once before, in Cherokee, North Carolina. We had visited a bear pit with black bears inside it. The noise was much the same.

For Yule 1993 a friend had given me a small black bear pendant because I always saw him as a large protective bear standing guard over me. He said that now, wherever I was, I would have a piece of him for protection. The pendant was lying in a small jewelry case near my head in the camper. Thanks to the animal, physical or nonphysical, for saving Bill's and Punks' lives. Love, light, life, and laughter.

—Judith A. Chadwell, Lafayette, Indiana
February 1995

Sacha

My daughter Elizabeth was born ten weeks prematurely with little hopes of survival. That night I went to my parents' home to report on her progress. Sacha, my mother's cat, was in the garden. I carried her into the house. Later Sacha got out and was run over. I was the last person to handle her or see her alive.

Every evening after visiting the hospital I phoned both my parents and my wife's parents to keep them up to date. My mother said that everything was going to be fine because the cat had appeared to her. Elizabeth was allowed home a few days later.

I continued to phone, though less often. One night my mother asked me to keep an eye on Elizabeth because she had dreamed about Sacha. She was sure that Sacha and Elizabeth were connected. The following day at work I received a message that Elizabeth had been taken to the hospital with a hernia.

From March 1978 until my mother's death in 1986, Mother often phoned me to say that the cat had appeared to her. This always happened just before Elizabeth came down with some minor childhood illness.

One night shortly before Elizabeth was due to begin eating solid foods, my mother called to say that the cat had appeared for quite a while, making Mother wonder if something serious was going to happen.

Elizabeth had to be hospitalized again. A pediatrics nurse was needed to help her cope with the change from milk to solid foods. Everyone was worried, but then the cat reappeared briefly. Elizabeth began to improve. She kept her food down, and she was discharged more quickly than we had expected.

Sacha appeared to warn us of every crisis in Elizabeth's life. The more serious it was, the longer the appearance. In the most serious cases Sacha always appeared to reassure us just before the climax of a crisis. My family now believes in spiritual guardians, although previously we were skeptical.

—Raymond M. Kelly, Durham, UK
April 1995

The Miracle Maker

I don't know his name, but his face will be etched in my mind forever. In the beginning I looked for him in our small town's shopping center, at grocery stores, at school and church gatherings—everywhere I went. He was hardly more than a whisper away from my every waking thought.

I asked about him, and described him to friends and strangers alike. He was a small man, clean-shaven, with thick, curly, brown hair under a canvas hat. There were deep lines in his weather-beaten face, which was burned to a deep brown. His blue eyes were so clear that the one time I looked into them, with fear in my own eyes, was like seeing a reflection of my soul.

I saw him once and only for a moment on a lonely blacktop Georgia highway. I was on my way home from a day of shopping with my mother and my three-year-old daughter. Suddenly my mom screamed, “She’s choking, she can’t breathe!”

I quickly pulled over to the side of the road, grabbed my baby from the back, and tried frantically to dislodge the piece of candy she had swallowed, but nothing worked. Mom and I were terrified. My little girl was turning blue and I knew we were going to lose her right there by the side of that long, desolate road.

But a miracle happened. Out of nowhere a man appeared. I turned around and found myself staring into his eyes. For one brief instant I felt I knew him. Without a word he took control. In a matter of seconds the candy flew from my daughter’s throat and she screamed as she gulped for air. While her grandmother and I hugged her and cried tears of joy, the man slipped away without a sound. I stood up to thank him, but he was gone. It was as if he had never been there at all. I looked in both directions and saw no sign of a car or anyone walking.

That was over 15 years ago and I have never been able to thank the stranger for that miracle. Many times I have wondered if he was an angel, sent to me in my greatest time of need. All I know for sure is that I owe this miracle maker a debt that I could never repay: I owe him the life of my child.

—M. L. Pezzuto, Maysville, Georgia
May 1995

Sam

In the fall of 1974 I had gone to a friend's house early in the evening to have some fun. A bunch of us from the factory were playing poker and drinking gin. By the end of the evening we were feeling pretty high.

The biggest gamble of the evening came when I decided that I was sober enough to drive home. I left my friends around 3:00 A.M. It was a dark autumn morning. Turning onto the highway, I noticed that the entrance ramp seemed a little different than normal. But I was tired and it was late, so I thought it was probably just my imagination.

Driving down the road, I noticed that some of the signs faced backward. "That's odd! They must be doing some more road construction," I reasoned.

As I approached a huge hill, a voice inside my head screamed, "Get over!" Then it was as if something beside me took over the control of the car. I could feel my hands turning the steering wheel toward the shoulder of the road. I could feel my foot applying the brakes, but I still did not know why.

Had I not pulled over, I would not have seen the truck and I surely would have had a head-on collision. I sat there shaking for some time. Then, I carefully made a U-turn and drove slowly home. That was also the last time I have ever driven after drinking.

Looking back on that night, it was obvious that I was not alone in my car. I believe that I have a guardian angel with a sense of humor. I call this angel Sam, short for Spunky Angel of Mercy. Since then I have been visited by this being many times. Sometimes he helps me and sometimes he plays pranks on me, like hiding things in our house. He never keeps things very long; just long enough to let us know he is there.

Many times I have emptied out the top drawer of my dresser when I was looking for something. Hours or even days later the missing object shows up in plain sight in the original drawer.

In December 1994 Sam woke me up in the middle of the night and told me to look in my check file. When I did, I noticed that there was a huge error, one that would have caused me financial disaster had I not caught it in time.

One evening a few months ago, I was sitting on the edge of my bed. I was flipping through the TV channels when someone grabbed me by the seat of my pants and pulled me backward. I turned around, but nobody was there.

Thank you, Sam. You are the reason I am here to write this article. You are the reason I have four fine children and a wonderful wife. And thank you for bringing back my stapler today. But you could have given it back yesterday, before I went out and bought a new one.

—Gregory Folsom, Kansas City, Kansas
November 1995

Helper in the Night

A stranger helped me out of a critical situation 16 years ago. My husband and I owned an antique shop. Every year we traveled to Pennsylvania to buy primitive pieces. Once we received a flyer from a man who was selling everything in his house and shop. We planned to go, and took off in high spirits. We spent our first night in Chambersburg, Pennsylvania. The next morning our truck would not start. A man came from a service station. He said it was the alternator belt.

"That's funny," my husband said. "I just put a new belt on it before we left on this trip."

However, the man from the service station put on the new belt and away we went. We arrived at the little town on top of a mountain where the sale was to be. There were many cars and trucks. I suggested we turn the truck around to head downhill because the road was unpaved.

The sale started and we bought some items. I noticed people looking down into the valley. It began raining but there was a beautiful rainbow all across the valley. Someone spoke, saying, "We're going to have a gully washer. I'm getting out of here."

We both got wet putting the things we bought into the truck. My husband tried to start the truck, but there was no spark. It was getting dark, there was no phone, and there was only one house on our side of the mountain. Everyone had gone and we didn't know what to do.

"There is only one thing to do—pray for God to send us some help," my husband said.

"Do you think God hears our prayers way up here, when it's black as pitch in the pouring rain? God doesn't even know we're here," I said.

"Let's try praying," he said.

We waited but there was no answer. We were certainly stuck, because the man that had held the sale was not coming back until the weather cleared.

"Let's try again. Pray and believe we'll get help," my husband said.

I leaned against the window and was almost asleep. Suddenly someone tapped on my window. I rolled it down. There stood a man in a black raincoat and hood. He asked, "Do you need help?"

My husband explained that the truck would not start. The stranger said, "Release the hood."

He walked around to the front of the truck, came

back to my side, and explained that the alternator belt was broken.

"What can we do?" my husband asked.

The stranger said that he knew where he could find a belt (my husband said that we'd never see him again). He thought the man lived around there because he didn't have a car.

In 20 minutes the man tapped on my window, asked us to release the hood, and walked around to the front of the truck. He came back and told us we were ready to go. When we asked what we owed him, he replied, "Nothing. Just help someone else in need."

I could not see his face and said, "This is the third belt we have replaced in two weeks."

He replied that we would never need another belt, and we never did. Years later, when the truck was sold after my husband died, the same belt was still on it.

How did he get up that slick road and put on the belt without light? I never saw his face and he did not want us to get out of the truck. I strained my eyes to look at the stranger, but all I saw was mist. He vanished into the night without a car or a light. Could he have been my guardian angel, my protector? Even my husband never mentioned the experience. All he would say was, "I don't believe it."

—Eaves Campbell, Charlotte, North Carolina
October 1994

The Angels Took Us In

Over the Fourth of July weekend in 1966 my husband Earl and I with our four children—Jim, Christina, Judy, and Shearlene—were traveling from Kansas City, Missouri, to visit our mothers in California. I was expecting another child in December. There was plenty of room for the children in the back of our Corvair Ranchwagon so the ride was fairly comfortable.

Just before we got to Wagon Mound, New Mexico, Earl got sleepy. He stopped and slept a while, then drove a few more miles and had to stop again. This was early in the evening and we were puzzled as to why he was so sleepy. We stopped for the last time in Wagon Mound and when Earl tried to start up the car again a wheel fell off.

We looked around for a garage but couldn't find one. We spotted a motel up the road and walked to it. There we were told another family had had similar problems and the motel was full. Here we were with four children, me pregnant, and no room in the inn!

The only thing we could do was go back to the car and wait for morning. Then a Mexican couple stopped to ask if they could help. The man said he worked for the railroad and pointed to a house beside the tracks we hadn't even noticed.

They invited the children and me to spend the night while my husband went for help. When we asked the names of our benefactors, they pointed to the mailbox with the name "Pedro Angel."

The house had no electricity, only coal oil lamps and a wood-burning stove, which we thought was very strange. Mrs. Angel cooked a delicious fried chicken dinner with mashed potatoes, gravy and hot biscuits with butter and honey. They showed us to feather-mattressed beds. The Angels apologized for the lack of modern conveniences saying this was all the railroad would provide. We found the lack of modern conveniences just marvelous! In the morning Mrs. Angel served us bacon and eggs and more biscuits and honey.

Earl could find no help to fix the car so we left the children with our dog Bob to guard them, and with the Angels looking in, I went with him to seek help. We finally managed to get the highway patrol to relay the broken part to Albuquerque, where a Chevrolet dealer opened his shop on the holiday to get the part with our promise to pay him when we got there. The highway patrol relayed the part back to us. By this time it was night again and the patrol turned on their lights while Earl repaired the wheel. All this time the Angels kept coming by to be sure we were all right. Finally, the car was repaired and we were on our way. We stopped and paid the dealer in Albuquerque. He invited us to dinner but we felt he had done enough for us already and declined the invitation.

The rest of the trip to California and back was uneventful but our experience had a surprising sequel. The following year we moved the entire family to California. The children and I traveled by train but Earl drove the Corvair with some of our belongings.

He stopped in Wagon Mound to see the Angels. To his surprise another family was living in the house by the tracks and said they had been there for three years. The house had electricity all through it and the "new" family living there claimed it always had.

Earl asked some of the other people we had spoken with the year before where the Angels were. Although some of them remembered him and had talked with him while the Angels were with him, no one knew the Angels or had ever heard of them!

We wrote to the railroad but they had no record of an employee named Angel. Still, my husband and the children and I know what happened and we never will forget the night the Angels took us in.

—Beverly Wilcox, Foothill Farms, California
December 1975

Amazing Animals

It is often said that dogs are man's best friend. Indeed, for thousands of years animals have lived with humans as livestock, guardians, and pets. The following stories demonstrate the strength of the intense bond that exists between humans and animals.

My Dog, Dick

Whenever dogs are mentioned, memory turns to my dog Dick, a Scotch shepherd of remarkable talents, and his part in saving my life when none but he could have known the danger.

My wife and children were visiting away from our Miami home one day in 1941. I came home to an empty house after a trying day and dropped into a chair near the fireplace with Dick lying at my feet. Utterly exhausted I fell asleep only to be aroused by Dick pulling at my trousers and making strange noises. He barked, growled, whined, and continually ran back and forth to the door. His behavior was so strange that I went to the door and stepped out on the porch. Dick indicated quite insistently that I follow him onto the lawn, and I did.

It was a beautiful cloudless summer night. The stars were bright and there was no sign of a breeze. Dick was standing at my side still shivering and whining when suddenly a blinding flash of lightning and a loud crash shook the ground. I was stunned for a moment but then I realized Dick was running in circles, yipping and barking and licking my hand.

While I was trying to quiet him a neighbor, William Blair, rushed over. Together we looked at my house and saw the chimney had fallen. Masonry was scattered over the roof and on the front steps. Inside we found the living room a shambles, full of debris from a large hole in the roof—and my chair was smashed. If I had been in that chair I would have been killed.

—Samuel Leigh, Miami, Florida
June 1969

Invisible Dog

As a child I owned a cocker spaniel that our family raised from puppyhood and which was my inseparable companion for some eight or nine years. The dog's name was "Chummy."

In the course of time Chummy passed away and I grew up and moved to another city where I was employed by a brokerage firm and resided with a private family, the head of which was a prominent auditor. The home of these good people was in a new, partially developed neighborhood and on the first day that I moved in with them, I decided to take an evening walk. Shortly after leaving the house I distinctly heard the pitter-patter of dog feet trotting along behind me.

Thinking it was the family dog, a female called "Lassie," I stopped and spoke to her but then observed that there was no animal in sight. I resumed my walk and immediately heard the tick-tack of paws upon the walk again. This was repeated several times and no matter how quickly I turned my head, I could discern nothing.

Puzzled, I returned to the house and related my experience to Mr. Dean, the auditor. He wanted to try the experiment with me and we left the house together. The same occurrence was repeated and Mr. Dean was soon convinced that a mystery existed. My auditor friend then suggested that I recall to mind some dog from my past that had possessed an unusual regard for me and of course Chummy came to mind at once. Spontaneously I called out in a firm but friendly voice, "Chummy, come here old boy." And my answer was a rushing of paws on the cement sidewalk right up to me, then a sound as of dancing up and down, just as Chummy used to greet me when I returned from school as a youngster.

I lived with the Deans for over a year and there never was a night that saw me on the sidewalks of the neighborhood which did not bring Chummy along as a constant companion. He would leave me if I got too near the more thickly populated area of the city and he would not be heard during a daytime stroll, but he always came at call under the usual favorable conditions and he took to walking at my side, rather than behind me, sometimes trotting on ahead or dropping back a bit as a dog will do, but never out of earshot. This phenomena was witnessed by several friends, though I must confess that those who came to scoff could hear nothing. Yet many heard as clearly as Mr. Dean and myself, nor was the sound faint and difficult to distinguish. It was a perfectly normal dog in every regard other than of sight and touch. When I moved away, Chummy and I lost each other again. I have not heard of, or should I say "from" him since.

—Jack Sheppard, Ecuador, South America
July 1950

Audrey's Miracle

In September of 1983, Dusty Krieg presented her stepdaughter with an adorable German shepherd puppy. Audrey was delighted. She has always loved animals, so it was not only a kind gesture on Dusty's part, it was a wise move to gain the acceptance and affection of a wary ten-year-old. My granddaughter Audrey had also gained a new brother, Michael, when her father remarried.

The newest member of the family was promptly named "Bear" because he resembled a cuddly teddy bear. I don't ordinarily favor dogs, but Bear captured my heart.

Bear spent his time exploring the nooks and crannies of the garage when Audrey was away, but dashed out to meet her or anyone else with great affection when they stopped in the driveway.

One Sunday while Audrey was visiting her mother, Dusty and Mike decided to run to the store. Bear normally would scamper into the garage if he saw someone head for a car. This time, however, he was fast on Michael's heels. Mike was not paying attention, and as he slammed the car door, he heard a sickening crunch and one horrible yelp. Bear's head was crushed, blood gushing from his mouth and ears.

Dusty ran into the house for a large bath towel and wrapped the puppy up in it before placing him in Mike's arms. They rushed him to a nearby vet, but the prognosis was not good. He advised them to put Bear to sleep. Dusty decided to take him home so Audrey could say goodbye.

When I answered my phone that Sunday evening, Audrey was sobbing as she related the day's events. She told me that her puppy was in a coma. "He doesn't move at all. He won't even open his eyes. Dusty says we are going to have to put him to sleep. What am I going to do, Nannie?"

"Audrey, please listen to me. Remember how we've always talked about God's healing energy being all around us?"

I could just see her nodding as she said, "Um-hmm...."

"Well, sweetie, just know that His healing power is right where you are now. When you get off the phone, go and pick Bear up. Hold him tenderly and just feel God's energy flowing from you to Bear. It is all around you, and in you, and flows from you. God loves all His creatures, Audrey—even a helpless, hurting animal. Bear is going to be just fine. Have faith. I'll be praying for both of you tonight. Okay?"

She seemed to be calmer so we ended our conversation. In my prayers, I asked our Father to be merciful and to please give us a miracle so that a little girl's faith could be strengthened.

The next afternoon I decided to stop by my son David's place before his daughter, Audrey, came home from school. As my car pulled to a stop in the driveway, a furry brown and white ball bounded out of the garage to greet me. It was Bear! I sat on the porch swing and picked the puppy up so that I could examine his head. There was no sign of any injury. He was licking my face with sloppy kisses when David appeared at the door.

"I thought I heard your car, and wondered what had happened to you. What in the world. . . ." His voice trailed off as he looked in disbelief at what he was seeing. "Mom, that can't be Bear. He was all but dead when I checked on him a couple hours ago."

Audrey rushed in from school a few minutes later. When she saw her pet, she fell on her knees—tears streaming down her face—as he greeted her with those special sloppy kisses. That smile was like sunshine filtering through her tears—the reward for another one of God's miracles.

When she related our conversation and her actions of the previous evening, her dad only nodded in acceptance. Growing up in our family, he was no stranger to apparent "miracles."

—Bernie Krieg, Terrell, Texas
June 1992

Four-Footed Angel

In April 1926, I visited my aunt, Mrs. Martin J. Secord, in Detroit. One Sunday afternoon it was arranged that I should go over to Windsor to visit friends there and that a mutual friend would pick me up at 8:30 P.M. and bring me home. I was there at the appointed hour—but the friend did not appear.

I waited until 11:30 P.M. and decided to try to get home by myself. I crossed on the ferry and boarded a streetcar. However, I suddenly realized that the worst was yet to come. After an hour's ride on the streetcar I would have to walk alone for three blocks through a tree-shaded residential district at considerably after midnight. I had been warned repeatedly of the danger for young girls out alone at night.

I became extremely frightened. I bowed my head and prayed. I asked God to protect me and please, not to let me walk alone. I prayed constantly and believingly and when my stop came I got off, alone.

Waiting expectantly at the stop was a dog. I spoke to him and he took his place by my side. He walked every step of the way home with me, then turned and trotted away. I never saw the dog again—he was certainly not a neighborhood dog.

A dog was probably the only protector that could have filled my need. I would have been terrified if a strange man or woman had appeared and offered to walk home with me. But I had complete confidence in the dog—which appeared to me to be of the breed known as a Boston Bull.

—Paula Crofton, Daytona Beach, Florida
October 1954

Unseen Protector

I was sightseeing in Havana, Cuba, on August 23, 1952. It was late at night and I had walked far from my hotel, down through the Prado and into a dark, quiet street in what I learned later was one of the worst sections of the city.

I wandered around partially lost when suddenly I realized that a big, rough-looking man was following me. I imagined he was after my money but of course I couldn't be sure. I turned into an alley and my pursuer turned into the alley also. I quickened my pace and he did likewise.

My heart sank as I realized I had run into a dead-end. A wall 20 feet high barred my escape. If only I had a dog, I thought in panic. In such an emergency I guess most persons think of guns or other weapons but I have great admiration for dogs and consider them capable of handling any situation. This seems to be the only explanation for what happened next.

As the man approached me, a knife gleaming in his hand, I felt the large bushy head of an animal move against my fingers. The head seemed to be that of a dog. I looked down and to my surprise could see nothing. I heard the animal growl and although I could not see it, evidently the man could. He stopped and shrank back into a doorway.

Then the invisible dog led me back through the dark streets to the bright lights of the Prado. When I was safe at the corner the bushy head I was holding disappeared.

I cannot express in words my stunned, thankful feeling toward the unseen creature that came to me in the dark streets of Havana and led me to safety.

—Graham C. Owen, Eau Gallie, Florida
October 1953

Wild Goose Story

I don't speak German, my ancestors aren't German, and no one spoke German to me when I was a baby.

Several years ago my husband and I became the caretakers of a dilapidated farm in tiny Medway, Massachusetts. We began to populate it with chickens, a bunny for our daughter Jessica, and a pair of baby geese, which the seller was almost sure were male and female. Gossie and Gander were always together and underfoot.

Winter arrived suddenly, covering every inch of grass with a foot of snow. Since my husband had taken a job out of town and only returned on weekends, the chickens and geese became my responsibility. Not wanting them to freeze, I spread some hay on the floor of one of the outbuildings and locked them in until the snow melted, going every day to give them food and water.

All went well for about three months, but without warning, Gander began to hiss at me. During this same week, I'd wake up in the morning with the words "Dach me Genser" running through my head. At first I thought nothing of it, but every morning for a whole week it was the same "Dach me Genser."

Finally I had a friend ask her mother, who was of German descent, if these words were German. "Yes," she said. "It means something about geese and a roof."

I remember Gander hissing and decided he was trying to tell me that they wanted to come out from under the roof. Since it was getting warmer, I let them out. The next day they started mating, and by Easter we had baby geese.

—Cathy Mann, Tuscon, Arizona
November 1992

Into the Pit

On an afternoon in the fall of 1975, I was hunting on state land outside Cazenovia, New York, with my elderly beagle Mitzi. The weather was sunny and crisp and the two of us leisurely ambled over the hills enjoying a fine late autumn day.

Suddenly I was practically paralyzed by a vivid internal vision of myself lying with a broken leg at the bottom of a deep pit in the freezing cold. As abruptly as it had come, the vision passed, leaving me puzzled and shaken. The warm sun and Mitzi's frantic jumping up on my legs snapped me out of it and I put the strange incident out of mind.

I wasn't too familiar with the area and later, as the sun and the temperature both started to drop, I searched for landmarks to lead us back to the car. We'd wandered so far that I was a bit disoriented and I started toward the top of a small hill to get my bearings. Mitzi, however, struck a fresh rabbit track and ran off yelping and howling down into a woods in a shallow valley. I followed and found my dog dug halfway into the tumbled-down foundation of an abandoned farmhouse. By the time I'd dragged Mitzi out, it was nighttime and pitch-black.

In the darkness the area was confusing and I couldn't recall the way out of the wooded valley, so I started walking at random. Mitzi, normally a sweet-tempered and dignified lady, stayed close to my heels until I'd walked perhaps 50 feet; then, to my utter astonishment, she growled at me. As I started to take another step forward, Mitzi bit me!

I stopped, of course, and clicked my lighter to see what was wrong. The flickering light showed, not more than two steps before me, an open pit which I later learned was the well that had served the abandoned farmhouse. Mitzi wiggled and pranced almost in apology and we slowly—and carefully—made our way to the top of the hill and then to the car. All the while I kept wondering if that afternoon my old friend Mitzi had shared my vision.

—James Rossano, Auburn, New York
January 1984

The Blessed Event

We acquired my beautiful blue great Dane, Tahoe of Impton, in Droitwich, Worcestershire, England, on February 13, 1971, when she was eight weeks old and brought her home to Duncan, Oklahoma, two weeks later. I planned to train her for both show and obedience. With daily grooming, long walks, bicycle runs, training, and going on errands with me, she never lacked for attention. I even baked special cookies for her as an occasional reward for good behavior.

A fresh batch of cookies went with Tahoe when family problems forced me to sell her in April 1973 to a breeder in Noble, Oklahoma. A couple of years later I learned about the uncanny way animals have of communicating with human beings.

On June 3, 1975, I was awakened about 4:00 A.M. to find Tahoe in my bedroom. She was excited and anxiously pacing back and forth as if she wanted me to follow her. She placed her powerful jaws over my hand and led me into the kitchen where she majestically walked to her bed and stood over her six puppies, four females and two males.

It was all a dream but so vivid and realistic that I awoke. I could still hear the sound of her paws and the newborn puppies' mewling. I actually went to the kitchen to see if Tahoe was there. Of course I had been dreaming; I returned to my bed and promptly fell deeply asleep again.

My bedside clock showed 5:20 A.M. when an agitated Tahoe came to my bedside and nudged me. I arose quickly and walked beside her to her bed; one female puppy and one male had died. This time I was actually in the kitchen when I became conscious enough to realize I had been dreaming.

Not having heard a word about Tahoe in the two years since I had sold her, I was surprised when a letter arrived from her new owner. The news was this: On the third of June at 4:05 A.M. Tahoe had given birth to six puppies, four females and two males. At 5:20 A.M. two puppies died, one female and one male.

—LaJunta Jewell, Duncan, Oklahoma
March 1984

Cats Can Understand

There are house cats, alley cats, and stray cats. Whitey was the latter. But if her origin was doubtful, her short wiry hair and insolent green eyes betrayed a Siamese strain. She roamed the canyon slopes around Topanga, California, begging handouts from inhabitants of the mountain cabins. This meager diet she supplemented with unwary field mice. That is, until her kittens arrived. This was in May, 1958, when I visited my daughter and her family in Topanga.

Tomassino, our arrogant and petted tomcat, was responsible for Whitey's litter. When she appeared each evening, alone, to share his meal he didn't dispute her right. But Tomassino became thin and irritable, for the mother cat greedily devoured the major portion of his daily ration.

Drastic measures were necessary to discourage these daily visits. Tomassino's dish of food was now placed behind the closed screen door of the porch. Whitey watched through the barrier indignantly, mewing plaintively, as he greedily lapped milk.

Where she had hidden her kittens was a mystery—and I was curious to see them. Talking down to her, through the screen, somehow our eyes locked in a curious communication.

"Go get your kittens," I commanded. "Bring them here. If you do, I'll give you food."

She turned and padded with determination toward a wooded area. Within the hour a commotion on the porch caused me to investigate. Mewing softly, reminding me of my promise, Whitey stood quietly, surrounded by five playfully romping balls of white fur.

—Margaret Grant, Santa Barbara, California
February 1960

Smiley, the Mystery Dog

My experience with an Alaskan husky has convinced me that pets can foretell death.

My mother passed away in April 1969 at age 76. She was a healthy, energetic woman who possessed a genuine enthusiasm for life unsurpassed by anyone half her age. Several months before she died, I sold my antiques business in Minneapolis and purchased a small house adjacent to her home in Floodwood, Minnesota.

One morning while I was installing new cabinets in the kitchen, I glanced out the window and saw a large white husky lying on the sidewalk. I opened the door and began talking to my visitor in a low, calm voice. He sat up and listened with his head tilted slightly to one side.

The poor, disheveled animal looked hungry and waited patiently until food and water were put before him. After eating his fill, he licked my hand to show his appreciation for this small kindness. The dog had one unique characteristic—one side of his lip curled slightly whenever he panted, giving him the appearance of smiling. He became known as "Smiley" from then on.

Where Smiley came from and why he chose my house was a mystery to us. The neighbors assumed he was a stray or had been abandoned by tourists passing through town. Three days after Smiley "adopted" me, I brought my mother her mail and some groceries she'd asked me to pick up. The breakfast dishes were still unwashed, and I found her lying on the sofa. From her ashen color and labored breathing, I knew she was quite ill. I called an ambulance and she was taken to the hospital. Later that afternoon, she was in a terrible condition.

At home that evening, after preparing a light supper, I sat down to watch television.

Smiley's usual place was on a rug by the door. But on this night he seemed nervous for some reason and finally settled down at my feet. He became preoccupied, dividing his time between watching the phone, glancing up at me, and whimpering. Around 9:00 P.M. I received a call: Mother had died peacefully in her sleep. As soon as I replaced the phone in its cradle, Smiley nuzzled my hand. His watery eyes seemed to say he was there to comfort me in my time of need. If I neglected to give him attention, he would tug at my trouser leg or find a stick and insist we play "fetch."

After Mother's funeral, I put my house up for sale. On the day the house was sold, Smiley gave me a long, wistful look as if this was his way of saying goodbye. When I returned from transferring the title, Smiley was gone. He disappeared as mysteriously as he appeared.

—Glen Kartin, Minneapolis, Minnesota
October 1999

Beagles Have Friends

We owned a Victorian cottage on Aqueduct Road in Schenectady, New York, during the late 1960s. It was unique in that it had an acre of ground yet was just outside the city limits. The house, green and white with a turret, was surrounded by trees and set on the rise of a hill. We named it Bonnie Dune.

My mother Jane Barrett and I were interested in the Ouija board and often tried to get messages with it. I never would have believed the reception we received from it one day as we worked with it in the spacious dining room at Bonnie Dune. We started this particular and memorable occasion on an early spring day in 1968. Mother asked if there were spirit friends present and the pointer quickly moved to "yes."

I asked the spirit to spell out its name but no name came. Instead the pointer spelled a jumbled plea for help. I watched the message unfold. I finally read,

"Help me, help me; I'm in a cage. I can't get out. I'm hungry." It paused for a few moments, then finished by spelling, "The man is mean."

We were both puzzled at the strange message and I asked, Where are you? Where is the cage? The reply came that the cage was close by and again the words "Help me."

The Ouija pointer then lay quiet and finally we put it away as the message was through and we became bored with waiting. I don't think my mother or I gave the message too much thought.

My grandmother Olive Peterman was living with us at that time and, being in her late seventies, liked to spend a good part of each day in a rocking chair gazing out of the dining room window.

About a week after our Ouija session she said she noticed that our neighbors in the nearby brick house had moved and she thought she saw two beagles in a pen at the side of the house. My grandmother always prided herself on her excellent eyesight and she said she wondered if the dogs had been abandoned as the house was no longer occupied.

We decided that this should be investigated. Mother, my brother Jim, and I walked over to the house. Sure enough, in a penned cage made of chicken wire were two young beagles without food or water. Both dogs were painfully thin. We made trips through the light spring snows to feed the dogs and after two weeks of no show from their former owners we removed them from their cage and found good homes for them both. Eventually the house was sold and the wire cage became a thing of the past.

I often have wondered about the Ouija's message that day and the plea for help that was the start of a strange mission of mercy from our Victorian cottage to the beagles' pen. If there are such things as spirit friends then surely those dogs had one.

—Jan Anclam, Schenectady, New York
March 1982

Our Psychic Mare

I was raised on a farm near the small town of Sulphur Springs in Yell County, Arkansas. It was beautiful country and our farm consisted of uncut timbers and fine cropland with a beautiful clear stream running through it.

In the late summer or early fall of 1908 I was only five, going on six. One bright clear day my mother Ida Shelton Rollans and I started out in the buggy to visit our sharecropper. I don't remember his name after all these years but he farmed our land called Shelton Farm in Logan County about 15 miles away. It was nearly harvesttime and we were going to see what our share would be from the farmer's harvest. I always loved any trips from home but especially one in that direction. We followed a back road through the Shoal Creek Narrows which cut three or four miles off the trip. This old road led through the tall timber and we always saw squirrels, deer, fox, raccoons, opossum, a variety of birds, and on occasion even bears and wild turkeys.

As usual Mother drove the small buggy with her special horse. Whenever Mother took the buggy we always used this particular gentle mare as she was very well behaved and Mother had no trouble with her. When we were about five miles from the sharecropper's farm the mare raised her head, snorted, and began to run. The sky was clear and no one was around; we couldn't understand the horse's strange behavior. Mother tried to get her under control but she just kept running down the middle of the road and would not stop.

Mother took me off the seat and put me on the buggy floor between her legs to keep me from bouncing out. The horse ran for a mile or so and as we neared a lane going to Mr. and Mrs. Clayborn Lasater's farm she turned in although Mother tried to keep her on the road. It was lunchtime and as we neared the house we saw the men coming in from the field. We were acquainted with the Lasaters and they insisted we stay and eat with them. After they unhitched the mare we went into the dining room.

Just as we were sitting down at the table we heard a loud roar. Everyone ran to the front porch. Catapulting down the mountain before us were trees, metal roofing, bedding, furniture, and other objects. It was a cyclone! As it came over the mountain it crossed the road right at the place where our mare had raised her head and started to run. We hurried to the storm cellar but didn't have to stay there long. The cyclone veered to the east and bypassed the house. Our mare had led us to safety.

—Virgil Shelton, Canton, Ohio
October 1975

Talking To Ants

"My God! Look at the ants all over my floor!" I exclaimed to my wife. "It's like a wall-to-wall ant rug!"

I don't know why, in 1966, the black ants decided to come into our house and infest our kitchen floor. But there were thousands of them.

Chlordane spray was legal as an insecticide at that time, so I filled a can with a diluted mixture and sprayed a blanket of my own right over the ants. I also crawled under the house and sprayed the water pipe leading from the ground into the kitchen, since many ants were climbing it into the house. I gave the crawl space a soaking with the chemical, sprayed the patio, the concrete step, and the back door.

The chemical has a strong odor so my family and I decided to leave the house for the afternoon, hoping that by the time we returned that night we would find a kitchen full of dead ants.

But when we did get home one look into the kitchen showed us the chlordane spray had been ineffective.

"What shall we do?" I asked my wife. "It doesn't seem to work. Maybe we had better check with an exterminator. Maybe they've got something stronger." My wife agreed and we decided I would have to call them.

While my wife was tucking our sons into bed I went downstairs to the kitchen to take one last look. The ants were still swarming all over the floor. Strangely enough, that is where they stayed. Not one ant had climbed up on the kitchen table, the counters, refrigerator, or other appliances. While I was pondering our predicament a thought suddenly struck me. Why not ask them to go away?

It seemed a ridiculous idea but I convinced myself I had nothing to lose. I moved to the center of the kitchen floor and squatted down—probably to make sure the ants could hear me. Clearing my throat I spoke in a voice slightly above a whisper; I didn't want my wife to hear me.

"Now, look here, you ants. God made you just like he made me. God's spirit is in you; otherwise you wouldn't have life. Now, as God's creatures you must learn that this house is for me and my family. You ants have your own abode and way of life. My family and I do not come and invade your home, do we?

"Now, I am asking that you please leave this house and go back to your anthills or wherever you live. My family and I will appreciate it if you leave as soon as possible—right now preferably. Thank you for listening."

I went to bed thinking, "How ridiculous!"

The next day was a beautiful Sunday, a spring morning. I took my time getting out of bed. I was not anxious to cope with our problem. But when I did go downstairs I found there was not a single ant in the kitchen. I hurriedly checked every corner. I went outdoors and checked the patio and back deck area. There were no ants anywhere. It was unbelievable! The ants had disappeared!

I ran upstairs, pulled my wife out of bed, and towed her downstairs. "Look. Take a close look," I commanded. "Do you see any ants? They are gone, gone, gone. . . ."

Our excitement awakened the children who came downstairs and joined in the jubilation.

We kept watch on our kitchen in the days afterwards but the ants never returned—not once in the 13 years we lived in that house on Apache Road in Westminster, California.

Did those thousands of black ants actually hear and understand my words? All I can say is that they were asked to leave and they left—for good. I have no explanation for this.

—Sebi Breci, Council Bluffs, Iowa
September 1982

Dolphins Are Psychic

In January 1991, my husband Charles Michael Deem and I spent a couple of warm winter days at the Monterey Beach Hotel, which sits on the beach in the bay. Historic Monterey is nestled along the curve of the bay, to the south of the hotel.

The coastal drop-off below the water line is quite steep, allowing large sea mammals unusually close access to the beach. We have a movie film, taken during another visit, of a young whale cavorting only yards from the hotel.

We were sitting on the sand between the hotel and the water, north of the hotel. A pod of eight dolphins swam by, passing close to the beach as they headed down the coast in a straight line. During the next two hours they passed by five more times, always swimming in a line parallel to the beach.

We discussed the dolphin experiments performed by various universities. In many ways dolphins are as intelligent as humans. A few scientists think they have the ability to communicate telepathically, so when the dolphins came into view for the sixth time, we tried our own experiment.

When they were several hundred feet away, we projected that they were beautiful, wondrous creatures and that we enjoyed watching the pod. I pictured the ancient stories of how they had saved the lives of sailors and told them I was sad that many of their kind had been slaughtered in tuna nets, and that I hoped man would continue to raise his consciousness where they were concerned.

We told them why they were special and intelligent: they maintain close family bonds throughout their lives, treat each other with respect, and live within their environment harmoniously. We told them that humans could learn from them. Most of all I projected a strong emotion of love. To prove they could hear us, we asked them to swim in a circle in front of us.

As soon as they were exactly before us, they broke out of their linear formation for the first time and swam in a tight circle. The entire pod circled before us. We were delighted and expressed our joy, projecting "Thank you." Then the pod swam in a line back up the coast in their original direction.

After six linear trips, why would the dolphins circle in front of us unless they "heard" our request and decided to fulfill it?

There was no other reason. No fishermen with bait, schools of fish, boats, or scuba divers. The only time in two hours that they circled was after we asked them to do it. Their elliptical laps were uniform and small, lasting 15 minutes, a long time for repetitive behavior. Animals exhibit sporadic or random actions unless they have a specific reason to be precise.

They swam with such joy! Other people walking on the beach stopped to watch and I wanted to shout that they were doing it because we had asked them to.

We are positive that they sensed our love and admiration and wanted to make us happy. It has been documented that captive dolphins will go to great lengths to please their human keepers. We won't ever forget that exuberant pod!

—Garrea Deem, San Jose, California
May 1993

"Wonder Horse" Sense

They tell me I was pale and shaken when I emerged from the dilapidated old barn that housed the famous "mind-reading" horse, Lady Wonder, who died recently from a heart attack at the age of 33. It was no wonder, for I had just had a most amazing experience.

Lady Wonder's quarters were even less elegant than an ordinary horse would boast. This unusual fact impressed me greatly as we drove up the muddy drive, which led to the farmhouse and the stable on Ruffin Road, on the outskirts of Richmond, Virginia. I reasoned that an animal possessed of the powers attributed to Lady Wonder certainly deserved ornate surroundings. I reasoned also that if she had predicted so many elections and races accurately, she should have gained a substantial monetary reward.

The car in which we arrived belonged to my cousin, who resided in Richmond. Deliberately we had left behind our own car, which bore Ohio license plates, our intention being to confuse the horse as much as possible. Oddly enough, my cousins never had visited the animal, in spite of all the favorable publicity it had received.

Lady Wonder's owner, Mrs. Claudia Fonda, an elderly woman who always was in attendance when the horse performed, ushered visitors into the barn, one at a time. They were permitted to write down three questions, to be answered by the horse, for a fee of one dollar. The questions were retained by the visitors, and neither the woman nor the horse came in contact with them. I questioned Mrs. Fonda, who explained that the writing was necessary to force concentration on only one subject at a time, since a fusion of several ideas might confuse the horse.

Lady Wonder had in front of her a large contraption, which I can best describe as a typewriter. When asked a question, she tripped the correct letters with her nose and spelled out the answer.

I was skeptical. Mrs. Fonda was very obliging when I requested that my three questions be answered without benefit of writing. I explained that I knew the importance of serious concentration, and would cooperate wholeheartedly. She seemed to sense that I was capable of doing exactly as I had promised, for she allowed me to ask my questions from memory.

My first question was rather ordinary. “What high school did I attend?”

Quickly, Lady Wonder tripped the phonetic spelling of “Lincoln,” for her alphabet was limited. This was indeed the name I had in mind, and I was mystified.

My second question was, “What is the city and state of my birth?”

This apparently was just routine for Lady Wonder, for she gave me the answer, “Cleveland, Ohio,” very quickly. Bear in mind, if you will, that we had nothing on our car or our clothing, to reveal our home state. With glee, I now contemplated my third question. This one, I was confident, would baffle the horse completely!

Before I divulge the third question, I must explain that I have a wonderful stepfather. My regard for him is shared also by my natural father. Both men have been very close to me, and if I had to make a choice, it would be a very difficult one.

With deliberate intent to confuse, I asked, “What is my father’s name?”

My thoughts were on both men; which one would the horse choose? I waited expectantly. Without hesitation she tripped the letters “BELOD.”

Mrs. Fonda clearly was puzzled. “Is—is that right?” she asked me in disbelief.

I must have turned pale for she appeared anxious. With humility, I stammered, “She couldn’t have done a better job!”

You see, my stepfather's name is Bernie, and my natural father has the unusual Czech name of Loddie. The horse had simply taken the first letters of each name and attached them together!

—A. K. Schreiner, Cleveland, Ohio
July 1957

The Truce of God

There is a legend that long before man came upon the earth all the animals spoke the same language and worshipped the same God. There was among them a cry of distress which all heeded. If an animal in trouble gave this cry, all the other animals would respect it and do him no harm. If a beast in final extremity made an outcry, there would be, no matter how hungry his attacker might be, a truce between them.

But when man came and killed, not because he was hungry but just for the pleasure of killing, the truce was neglected for man did not know the call and did not recognize it. So animals forgot it almost altogether and the truce of God is no more.

I had an experience once that brought forcibly to my mind the old story. It was on a winter day in 1942 after a heavy snowfall. I was staying at a farm near Wynot, Cedar County, Nebraska, five miles from the Missouri River.

On such a day there is no greater sport than rabbit hunting. I put on my snow boots, took my gun, called the two farm dogs, and started out. The day was perfect; no sharp wind, but not enough warmth to start a thaw. The snow lay like a great sheet over the land, blotting out familiar signs and making the world seem strange and new.

The dogs plunged through the snow, which was soft and deep enough to retard their movements a little but they were big strong dogs and enthusiastic hunters. Soon they flushed a big jackrabbit from the edge of a cornfield. He came out of some brush in the fencerow, bounding high and coming down only to rise again in a smother of snow several feet away. The dogs gave tongue at once and they were enjoying the chase so much that I did not shoot, though the rabbit made a good target.

Straight up the hill they went, the rabbit well in the lead but the dogs following eagerly. I could hear their excited barking long after they went over the hill out of sight.

Then the world was quite still. Not a shadow moved, not a bird flew across the white expanse. I stood quietly, enjoying the serenity and peace of the day. I do not know how long I waited there until I became conscious of the distant barking of the dogs. It grew louder; they were obviously headed back toward their starting point.

I saw a dot moving on the hill's crest; it grew larger as I watched until it became the rabbit, still leading his pursuers but not by any great distance. His jumps wavered as he came nearer; the soft snow made difficult going. He apparently was so exhausted that he did not notice me standing by the fencerow for his last desperate leap carried him to within 10 feet of where I stood. He fell at the edge of the field and could not rise again.

The dogs were almost upon him when he lifted his head a little and cried out. It was not like any sound I have ever heard before. It was high, harsh, and piercing, sustained and swelling. I was astounded that so small a beast could make so great a sound. It ceased abruptly and the rabbit's head fell back upon the snow. But the two dogs stopped where they stood. They sat down in the snow, panting a little, watching the rabbit whose sides were heaving as he regained his spent strength.

They sat there for at least five minutes. Then the rabbit got up slowly and made a try at bounding through the snow. His progress was pitiful but he kept moving while the dogs watched attentively.

He reached the cover of the fence brush and disappeared.

Then the dogs came over to me, wagging their tails to tell me they were ready to go hunting again.

I went with them, my gun heavy on my shoulder, for now I was going just for a walk in the winter snow. Somehow I no longer felt like shooting rabbits.

—Magdalene Craft Radke, Lincoln, Nebraska
October 1954

Family Ties

Blood is thicker than water, the saying goes, and family members stick together through good times and bad, sharing the joys and sorrows of their lives together. Sometimes this familial bond is so strong that messages can travel across time and space to alert, comfort, or reassure family members when a loved one is hurt or in danger. And in some cases, the bond is strong enough to relay a message from beyond the grave.

Visit From Beyond

Several years ago, my wife and I lost our one-year-old firstborn in an accident which also took the life of my mother. My wife and I escaped with cuts and bruises.

My wife mourned our baby until it became an obsession, so to get away from familiar sights, such as the nursery, mother's room and belongings, we took a house in the country.

Everything worked out fine and my wife seemed to be recovering quite well.

One evening we were sitting before the fireplace, chatting and listening to some old records on the phonograph when the wind blew the front door open. It made an eerie sound as it came through the reception hall.

"Must be a storm brewing, the way the wind howls," I said as I went out and closed the door. "My goodness! It's such a damp cold feeling, maybe it's getting ready for a first snowfall."

I sat down beside my wife on a davenport before the fire.

Immediately the door blew open again and a gust of wind blew out the only lamp in the living room.

I fumbled in my pockets to find a match, when my wife said, "Look, Jim, over there by the door!" There was a white shadowy outline that seemed to be moving toward us.

Needless to say we were frightened. I put my arm about my wife's shoulders and held her tightly to me. All at once there was a flash of light and there stood Mother with our baby in her arms.

"Oh! Mother!" My wife collapsed in my arms as she spoke. I wondered if I were having a dream! I shook my head.

"Jim," the vision spoke. "Tell Kathy not to worry about little Jimmy. I will take care of him. We are very happy in our heavenly home. Goodbye, my son." The light slowly faded and the vision went with it, leaving us in complete darkness.

I put my wife on the davenport and lit the lamp. I was shaking from head to foot. I went to the kitchen and got a glass of water. When I returned, my wife was opening her eyes. I gave her a drink and took her in my arms.

"What happened, Jim?" she asked, weakly. "I thought I saw Mother with little Jimmy in her arms." She looked at me with a question in her eyes.

I wanted to spare her, yet felt that she should know the truth. "We saw a vision, darling. It was mother. She doesn't want us to worry about Jimmy anymore, as he is safe with her in heaven." The vision cured my wife's grief.

—M. E. H., Flint, Michigan
Fall 1948

A Loving Call From Beyond

It was October 1978, and as I looked out the windows of my apartment all I could see were the treetops swaying fiercely from the strong, howling winds. The rain was so strong that I thought the windows would break. The sky was dark and dreary, and each boom of thunder sent chills through my body.

My husband, Nickie, and I were preparing to attend a family get-together 60 miles away. I was a bit apprehensive about the hour and a half ride that lay before us.

My husband was waiting for a business telephone call which was due any second, and we were to leave immediately thereafter.

When the phone rang I answered it, but to my utter surprise, it was for me and not my husband. On the other end was my grandfather, Herman Meritz. I was speechless because my grandfather had died two months earlier! When he spoke to me, the background was quiet but at the same time, distant. When he asked to speak to me by name, I was horror-stricken. I thought it had to be a mistake.

When I asked him again who he was trying to reach, he said, "Randi, my granddaughter."

He told me my phone number and that I had been married about five years and lived in an apartment with no children and was such a pretty girl. He said he missed me and wanted to talk to me. And then he said, "Don't you know my voice?"

I told him again that he must have a wrong number because I didn't understand how this could be happening. After a moment of silence, he said he was sorry to have troubled me. Through my tears I told him he was not trouble at all, and that I hoped he found his granddaughter. He sadly said goodbye and faded away to nothingness.

There was no click that you normally hear when someone hangs up the phone.

When my husband came into the living room, I was curled up on the floor crying, with the telephone in my hand. From the moment the connection was broken, I realized it most definitely was my grandfather. All I could think was, "Why was I so stubborn as to be a disbeliever?"

I've been told that I have psychic abilities, and that's why he was able to contact me because I was probably more receptive to the world beyond. I've prayed and prayed since that phone call that he would call me again because now I'm ready to communicate with him. I'm sure he knows that I miss him very much and think of him all the time.

And, who knows, maybe my prayers will someday be answered.

"I'm ready now, Pop, so please, please call me!"

—Randi L. Biba, Philadelphia, Pennsylvania
April 1992

A Silent Cry

In January 1982, my youngest child Charlene was nine years old. On the fourteenth of that month I was out in the backyard hanging laundry when suddenly, in my head, I heard Charlene scream, "Mommy!" It was not a real sound but I knew something was wrong.

I dropped the shirt I was hanging and ran toward the barn where my husband Tony was fixing a fence. As I reached him our horse, riderless, charged past.

"Was Charlene riding?" I asked. Tony thought not but somehow I knew my daughter must have been thrown.

"Charlene is hurt!" I yelled. I started across the field with Tony right behind me and about halfway across, we found Charlene unconscious on the ground. Her injuries were minor, thank God, but she had to spend one night in the hospital.

I often wonder how long she would have lain there if I hadn't heard her "call."

—Kathryn Sperske, Campo, California
July 1984

The 25 Pumpkin Seeds

In the spring of 1900 while we lived in the village of Tustenky Galicia, Austria, my mother became seriously ill. I was then seven years old.

After the doctor examined my mother I overheard his brusque verdict as he stood looking down at her. "You'll never live to sail to America to join your husband for you will die very shortly."

I heard my mother reply in a feeble voice, "God holds in His hand all the tomorrows; the future is His."

I was especially tired that night after performing the nursing chores, as well as mentally confused, but I could not sleep. I lay awake, pondering my mother's statement and hating the doctor for his tactless prediction. As I stared into the darkness I saw a white-shrouded form emerge from the wardrobe closet opposite my bed and approach me.

I tried to speak but could not utter a word. I gazed open-mouthed at the figure which I now saw to be that of a woman. She introduced herself as my maternal grandmother, Sarah. Taking my hand, she said, "Here are some pumpkin seeds. Know that as many of them as I leave with you, which number in all 25, so many years will your mother live from here on."

Then she patted my hand and with a chuckle walked backwards to the wardrobe closet and disappeared. I clenched my hand tightly around the seeds and, somehow calmed by my experience, I fell asleep.

I woke early the next morning and found my mother in a cheerful mood. I told her of my experience and from my description of the vision, including the slight lisp with which it had spoken, my mother was convinced that Grandmother Sarah had appeared to me. I had never seen my grandmother while she was alive. She had died many years before I was born.

I was disappointed over not being able to find the pumpkin seeds but my mother consoled me with the explanation that they were invisible to the living.

According to the vision's promise, my mother recovered and we sailed to the United States. Twenty-five years later, in 1925, my mother died.

—Pauline Morgenthal, Bronx, New York
April 1954

Off the Deep End

My brother George, my daughter Trina, and I were hot and tired after driving all day in August 1977 on our way to Florida. We stopped at the South Carolina border to spend the night and rented a second-floor room in a hotel. Trina was four years old and impatient to get into the swimming pool. I carefully showed her the baby pool to the left of the large adult pool and told her I would be with her in a minute. There were 30 or 40 people in and around the pool, so I thought she would be completely safe.

My brother lay on one of the double beds in the room watching TV. I grabbed my bathing suit from my suitcase and entered the small windowless bathroom and closed the door, at the same time starting to unbutton my blouse.

Suddenly the bathroom cubicle seemed airless; I felt an eerie stillness. After a second I heard a voice saying, "Help! Help me!" With no knowledge of why or what was happening I ran out of the tiny room and past my startled brother, screaming, "Help her! Help her! She's drowning, for God's sake!"

People stared as I ran screaming toward the pool area. Then a dark-haired man who had been sitting in a lounge chair dove into the 10-foot depth of the blue water and brought my daughter to the surface. I grabbed her from his arms, sobbing and thanking God and the kind man who had saved her.

Trina looked up at me and said, "Mommy, I was calling for help under the water but nobody heard me!"

I hugged her wet little body and whispered, "I heard you, baby. I heard you."

—Nancy A. LaFrance, West Palm Beach, Florida
April 1982

The Dreams Are Over

One day in 1969, when my son Jon was 12 years old, I answered the bell to find his sixth-grade teacher standing at the door with his hand on Jon's shoulder. My son's forehead was bandaged. "He fell in gym," the teacher said. "The emergency room patched him up and we gave him the day off." I thanked him and

Jon came inside and sat down in front of the TV.

As I dusted the floors I smiled to myself. I had dreamed this exact accident three nights before. All of Jon's life I had had prophetic dreams of any trouble ahead for him. I had told my daughter Ann about my dream and I knew she would be interested to hear that once again my dream had come true.

Two years later, in 1971, I again dreamed about Jon. I saw my son dead in an auto accident. He was the driver. This dream bothered me but it would be years before Jon could drive.

In the dream I saw the car piled up against a tree and my son dying in an ambulance. I began to pray. Somehow I got into the ambulance and knelt beside Jon. Life was leaving his body and I was praying for his soul. He gasped and died. Suddenly the breath seemed to leave my body; I couldn't breathe. I gasped for air and woke. I was screaming, "Jon is dead!"

My husband shook me back to reality and assured me over and over that it was only a dream.

But the dream stayed with me; I had seen every detail of the scene where my son died. I had felt "his" life leave my body.

When Jon was 21, I was visiting friends away from home. One of them was leaving that day for Europe and we were all excited and cheerful about the trip. The doorbell rang but I paid no attention and went on doing my hair.

My hostess came into the room. "Your husband is here," she said in a soft voice. There was an atmosphere of absolute stillness in the house as I went into the front hall.

"Jon is dead," my husband said. He began to tell me about the auto accident.

Jon and some of his friends had been out for the evening in two cars. They were taking one fellow home, driving on an almost straight stretch of country road, when the car Jon was driving left the pavement, after hitting the shoulder of the road, and rammed into a tree. The estimated speed was over 80 miles an hour. Jon was DOA at the hospital; the date was June 21, 1979.

I heard the police report; I saw the pictures of the accident scene; I went to the spot where the car had crashed. In every detail it was as I had dreamed it eight years before.

Since there actually is no time or space, perhaps I was there with Jon on that night he died.

—Patricia Woody, Rockford, Illinois
August 1982

Deathbed Visit

In what could have been a dream I stood at the foot of my grandparents' bed. My grandmother Bea Goldman was reading a book and my grandfather Ben appeared to be asleep. They were not aware of my presence. But as I stood there observing them my grandmother said something to my grandfather. When he did not reply she turned to look at him and realized that he was not breathing. She shook him and discovered that he was dead.

At this point I suddenly sat upright in my own bed on the other side of Atlantic City, wide awake. Looking at my clock I found it was midnight. Not wishing to disturb my parents I decided to wait until morning to tell them about my astral dream trip.

The next morning, October 4, 1961, I had risen and was getting ready for school when Mother came in and told me the news of my grandfather's death the night before.

Later in the day I heard my grandmother tell what had happened and she described Grandfather's death exactly as I had seen it during the night.

—Marian Banks, Venice, California
July 1975

The Lady is Dead

Great-aunt Maude Flint's picture had stood on the same spot as long as my four-year-old son Jimmy could remember. Auntie Maude never had come east from Oregon but I had corresponded with her since childhood and we had worked up a close relationship through our letters. Auntie Maude was a Spiritualist while I was a stout disbeliever.

One day in 1925 we had just finished lunch when Jimmy walked into the living room and picked up Auntie Maude's picture.

"Mama," he said, "the lady is dead."

I quickly took the picture from him and said, "No, dear, Auntie Maude is very much alive. Whatever made you say such a thing?"

"Because she is dead," he insisted. "I know it."

A cold tingle went up and down my spine. "Jimmy," I ordered, "I don't want to hear you say that again."

Then the phone rang. It was Corvallis, Oregon calling. Great-aunt Maude had died unexpectedly a short time before the call.

—Dorothy Reed, Clearwater, Florida
April 1975

Keep the Candle Burning

My brother Gary joined the Marines in 1968 and was sent to Vietnam in 1969. Because he was there and because many of my friends were being shipped over there, Vietnam was much in my thoughts.

Gary had been overseas about a month when I had a peculiar dream. It seemed as if a spirit entered my bedroom, a spirit that filled me with love, so I felt no fear when it spoke. The spirit told me there was something I could do for my brother: I was to get a picture of him and light a candle every day in front of the picture. The spirit said Gary would feel the warmth and love coming from home and would be helped to return safely.

From that day forward I kept a candle burning in front of a picture of Gary. Soon a letter came from him saying that despite the distance between us he felt close to home. When I replied I told him about my dream and what the spirit had told me to do. His letters thereafter always ended, "Keep the candle burning."

One day about the middle of August 1969, I was alarmed to see the candle flickering. Finally it went out completely. This made me certain my brother was in trouble. While I napped that afternoon my dream spirit reappeared. It told me, "Your brother lives but he has been wounded in the knee." I called my parents Homer and Mildred Benson and told them the message I had received. The next day from the Red Cross they received official notification that he had been wounded in the knee.

The next time the candle acted up was in October. The flame dropped low and remained low for two days. During this period the spirit came to me again and said, "Your brother lives but he is sick." I called my parents to warn them to expect bad news and within a few days a letter came from Gary saying that his illness had been diagnosed as malaria on October 12. The candle let us know when he had a relapse in November and also when he became so ill in January 1970 that he was sent home.

—Tyrone Benson, St. Louis, Missouri
January 1977

A Stomach Pain

On August 6, 1976, my friend, Dorothy, and I were driving to a small commune called Ananda. We decided to camp rather than use a motel.

We parked by a field. Dorothy prepared to sleep in the car. I hauled my sleeping bag outdoors. As I bent down to stretch out the sleeping bag, I doubled over with cramps. The pain went through my entire body for a minute or so. Finally I was able to straighten up again. As the pain receded, I relaxed and went to sleep.

The following day we arrived at the Ananda Commune. We were assigned our bunks in the guest house and unloaded the car.

A man walked up to us and asked, "Are you Ruth Kaufman?"

I was amazed. I had told no one where we were heading. The gentleman told me that Jacob Kaufman, my husband, asked for me. He said, "There is no phone available in the area."

"Dorothy, I have four children. I wonder what happened to them?" I said anxiously to my friend.

She remarked that it was too far for me to go to a phone and drive back. My gas tank was low. "I'll stay here. You travel on, but let me know what happened," she told me.

After several miles I located a pay phone. I tried to get through to my home with no success. The phone was not working.

Finally I knocked on a farmhouse door. The two children had mouths smeared with blue from the blueberry jam their mother was making. She granted me permission to use the phone.

My husband answered. My daughters, Nita and Wendy, were in an accident in Jylland, Denmark. The man driving them to an art exhibit in a little Renault smashed into a car parked along the side of the road and both sisters were thrown out of the car onto the pavement. Wendy had died.

"What should I do with her body?" he asked sadly.

"I'll call you back in the morning," was all I could say.

The woman hugged me against her full bosom while I cried. The pain in my stomach had happened simultaneously with Wendy's death.

Nita, 26, had brain damage and spent subsequent months in the hospital. She is alive today and living in New York. Wendy has spoken to me through a medium and I have the message on tape.

—Ruth Kaufman, Fairbanks, Alaska
September 1993

Dad

Back in 1963, while waking up from surgery in a hospital bed, I felt a hand touch my arm ever so gently. I rolled over and looked toward the chair near the corner of my bed. There sat my father, dressed in pale green pajamas and a plaid bathrobe. Dad looked tired and troubled. Then he smiled and faded away.

When my husband came to visit, I told him of my experience. He didn't make any comment at the time, which I found odd.

While driving home several days later, my husband pulled the car to the curb, shut off the engine, and began talking. The doctor had forbade him to tell me, in my condition, that my father had had a heart attack and was rushed to the hospital. It turned out that this happened at exactly the same time he appeared to me, 300 miles away. Dad survived and shared our lives for another 15 years.

—Donna Ballman, Cedar Grove, Wisconsin
October 1999

Mother Touch

During World War II on a freighter in the mid-Atlantic I had my first encounter with the supernatural. Our engine had broken down about eight days out of Halifax and the convoy had left us far behind. The crew was tense and jumpy for the waters were dangerous with enemy submarines and our guns could afford little protection in case of attack.

On the third day at sea I lay in my bunk sleeping before my next watch. There was no one else in the quarters. During my sleep I had the very odd sensation that a warm hand was touching my arm. I opened my eyes and saw a figure the sight of which almost paralyzed me. It was that of my mother—who had passed away over 10 years before!

Nothing was said, no movement made, but before I could rise the apparition disappeared. Needless to say I got out of that bunk-room as fast as I could.

Down in the engine room the engineers and wipers were still trying to repair the engine. I went down below, to be around people and lights. The fireman started to say something to me, but a deafening explosion and a great lurch of the ship sent us all sprawling.

The lights went out and we knew we had been hit by a torpedo. Somehow we made our way safely out of that deathtrap by the guidance of the phosphorescent signs placed about the engine room and other parts of the ship.

A few moments later the crew was sardined in lifeboats, rowing quickly away from the slowly sinking vessel. All the crew were accounted for in the lifeboats except one messman who had jumped over the side.

Looking back at the vessel broadside I saw a great gaping hole in its starboard side where the torpedo had struck midship. Directly above this hole, where I had been asleep in my quarters a few minutes before, was a tangled mass of steel and wood that would have meant my end had I continued to sleep there. My mother had waked me only just in time.

—J. Michnovich, Toronto, Canada
November-December 1951

What Saved the Baby?

It was a July summer evening in Martha's Vineyard, a little island off the Cape Cod coast of Massachusetts. My husband and I, the new parents of our first child, a daughter, were on our way to a neighbor's house. It would be the first time I had been able to dine out this summer and the Kinsburys, old friends with three children of their own, had said they would care for our little girl.

"Go on out and have fun, honey," the more experienced mother told me. "Don't worry about a thing. I'll put the baby right in our baby carriage in my room here."

So my husband and I went to a local restaurant and ordered a large swordfish steak dinner, preceded by one cocktail. Everything should have been strictly happy and gay but as I lifted the cocktail glass to my lips an intangible terror came over me and I put it back on the table.

"What's the matter?" asked my husband. "Don't you feel well? Shall I cancel the dinner?"

"Something is wrong with the baby," I said. "I've got to call the Kinsburys."

"Don't overdo this Mother stuff," my husband teased. "Mrs. Kinsbury has raised three kids of her own and you haven't even started."

Forcing myself to smile, I again picked up the cocktail glass. It was pretty silly to worry about my daughter when she was with reliable people. Also, a husband must not think that his wife couldn't go out and be gay, like old times, without always worrying.

But the feeling persisted. In fact it became so violent that I felt as if I could hardly breathe. No human being on earth, no ridicule, nothing could stop me now. Without a word to my husband I leapt from the table and ran to the telephone booth. It had a gabby sailor inside. It was the only phone nearby, so I pounded and pounded on the door. With a sour epithet the sailor finally hung up and departed. It was exactly seven when I tore into the telephone booth and gave the Kinsbury's number. It rang four times.

"Sorry, no answer," the operator said.

"Try it again, I know somebody is there," I said.

The operator rang again and it signaled busy. For 10 frantic minutes the line either signaled busy or didn't answer. Finally, limp with exhaustion and terror, I went back to the table. Then an odd thing happened. I had been in the phone booth since exactly seven o'clock. Now at seven-thirty I felt giddy with relief. Whatever had happened was all right—but I still must call the Kinsburys or go there.

"Try phoning one more time," my husband said. "After all we've ordered the food and it must be just something wrong with the phone. You know the Kinsburys would never go off and leave our baby, let alone three of their own."

I tried once more and Mrs. Kinsbury answered the phone.

"Oh, am I glad to get you," I cried. "I know you'll think I'm neurotic or nuts, but is my baby all right?"

"She's okay now," Mrs. Kinsbury said, "but it sure gave us a turn. The phone rang at seven—"

"That was me," I said, "but you didn't answer."

"I know. Wait a minute. The phone rang at seven—I just happened to look at the clock because I knew the baby would need to have a bottle soon—and then I thought I would go and look at the child before I got gabbing with some neighbor. When I got into the room the baby had rocked the carriage back and forth so that a pile of blankets on the end of my bed had fallen in on top of her. She was smothering. She was purple—had foam all over her mouth and face. The phone was still ringing but I screamed for my husband. He gave the baby artificial respiration, and then the phone stopped ringing just long enough for me to call the doctor. He came and the baby is all right now. I was just going to call you when the phone rang again."

We hurried back to the Kinsburys and I picked up the baby I had so nearly lost and held her until she went to sleep.

"I don't understand how you happened to call," Mrs. Kinsbury said. "Ordinarily I'm capable of taking care of a baby. I don't know why I decided to look at her before I answered the phone."

"It was because I wanted you to," I said. "If you had answered the phone I was going to tell you to look at the baby right away, even if you thought I was crazy. Something told me the baby needed help."

—Faith Clarke, Honolulu, Hawaii
April–May 1952

To Be or Not to Be

In March 1907 my parents lived in the small town of Parson, Kansas. My mother had married at age 16, and by 19 she was pregnant for the third time, with me. My father's sister, Ora, had just had an abortion by a local doctor, and she had convinced my mother to do the same. An appointment was made for Monday morning.

On Sunday, one day before Mom was to go, my family had a potluck dinner, followed by a taffy pull in my grandmother's backyard. Everyone was having fun, especially when Ora began showing her teeth and pointing to them, saying "m-m-mmm."

It had seemed so funny. Everyone laughed, thinking it was because of the taffy, but after a bit they realized it was not funny and that something was seriously wrong. Ora was taken home and a doctor was called. At 10:00 P.M. she died of lockjaw.

At exactly the same time, Mother said she had just turned out the light to go to bed, and as she turned, she saw Ora standing in a bright light. Ora held out her hand toward my mother and said, "May, don't!" Then she faded.

Mom screamed and fainted. Dad ran into the room and, when Mom revived, she told him what had happened. She also told him about her pregnancy, since she hadn't done so before, and about her appointment the following day. Dad took her in his arms and made her promise never to do such a thing again.

My mother told me this story when I was pregnant with my first child and said, "Of my five children, you are the one who has given me the most pleasure. You have never caused me one tear or heartache, and you have given me only happiness. To think that you might never have been!"

—Genevieve E. Nichols, Los Angeles, California
August 1995

The Substitute

By the spring of 1936 multiple sclerosis had taken from me the power to walk. On October 10 that year I lay in my twilight-darkened bedroom in our home in Redgranite, Wisconsin, knowing little more than that my mother and father were sitting beside my bed. I heard Mother's voice as if from a distance saying, "We must call Dr. Beck. He won't be able to get here from Wautoma until 10 o'clock." I heard a door close; then all was quiet.

From some distant realm came music and a kaleidoscopic glow of light. Slowly my body seemed to float up toward the light. I heard a voice—my aunt Ella Christenson's voice—saying, "I'll go in place of her."

Although I could not see Aunt Ella I knew she was talking directly to me when she said, "When the doctor comes, have him come to my house."

Slowly the light dimmed and melted into the lamplight of my room. I felt a new buoyancy and the semicoma seemed to lift. When the doctor finally arrived at my bedside I was feeling better than I had for weeks.

I couldn't tell the doctor that my aunt needed him without arousing a curiosity and questions that I couldn't satisfy, so I remained quiet.

Three days later dogs howling near my Aunt Ella's house not far from ours in Redgranite disturbed the neighbors. When she did not answer her doorbell, they had to break into the house. They found Aunt Ella dead. She had suffered from myocarditis and the doctors verified her fatal heart attack had occurred at approximately the time I heard her voice on the night of October 10, 1936.

—Kathleen Knutson, Redgranite, Wisconsin
July 1969

A Daughter's Love

It was not until the death of my daughter, which occurred on her fifteenth birthday, that I began to question seriously and longingly, "Where are the dead?" Should anyone have told me at the time of her death that she would return to me again, I would have thought them insane and would have paid little attention to their remarks.

The fact that her return was over such a seemingly insignificant incident and that it was witnessed by my son also, makes it all the more perplexing to me. Thoughts of that never-to-be-forgotten night fill me with sadness and confusion.

A friend of mine had presented me with a beautiful gold necklace which was set with a large pearl. I had always been an admirer of jewelry of any sort and naturally I was very proud of this gift and wore it every day to work. But the fact that I considered it about two inches too long worried me considerably and I had remarked to my son that when I felt financially able I would have it shortened.

It was my custom to take it off over my head and it was while I was removing it one night, preparatory to retiring, that the chain broke in several places. I remarked to my son, who witnessed the breaking of my necklace, that I was unable to have it repaired, but would do so when I received my next salary check, which was about a week distant, and that I would at this time have it shortened. With this remark I picked up the broken chain, placed it in an envelope, sealed it, and tucked it securely in my purse. The following morning I took it to work with me.

That evening a friend telephoned me and invited me to attend the theater with her, and I accepted the invitation. After the show we stopped in a nearby cafeteria for a light lunch. While there I told her I wanted to show her a necklace I had recently received but that I had broken the chain the night before. Imagine, if you can, my surprise when I tore the envelope open and pulled out the necklace in perfect condition. Not only was the chain repaired, but it was about two inches shorter.

I was too filled with my own thoughts to offer any explanation, and in fact, I had none to offer. Thinking that perhaps she had not heard my remark that the chain was broken I said nothing about it. She was filled with admiration of the beautiful pearl.

My son and I were at that time boarding with a friend of ours and shared a room together. It was a large room with two front windows and the furniture consisted of two single beds, two chairs, a table, and an old-fashioned wardrobe. A small dressing room adjoined it.

When I arrived home my son was busy with his studies. We talked for almost an hour, most of which time was consumed in trying to solve the mystery of the repaired necklace. Finally, weary and finding no solution, we decided to retire.

It was a beautiful moonlit night and the streetlight in front of our window was not needed for the scene we were about to witness. No sooner had I turned out the light and flung my weary body on the bed than my daughter appeared. She stood by my bed, radiantly beautiful, her golden hair falling over her face. I shall never forget the three short sentences she slowly uttered and her mystifying disappearance. Standing directly in front of me and wearing the same dress I selected for her burial, she said, "Mother, I fixed your necklace. I think it is very beautiful. Wear it always."

I reached out my hand to touch her, only to find that she had vanished as mysteriously as she had entered.

My son, who quickly recognized his sister's voice, had by that time gotten out of bed. I turned on the light and saw that he was very pale.

"Mother," he said, "did you see and hear Mary Lee?" He seemed dazed and I thought he might be dreaming. I told him that she had been there; that I saw and heard her and together we tried to solve the mystery. He remarked that he thought the place must be haunted and that he was in favor of moving. Needless to say, neither of us slept that night.

The following morning I showed the repaired necklace to the jeweler in the building where I worked. I related my story to him and he assured me, after careful examination of the necklace, that human hands could not have repaired it, for there was not a trace of where the links had been united. The chain was a thick one and one that would be very difficult to repair without a trace of where the links were put together.

—Estelle Finnegan, St. Louis, Missouri
September 1949

Good Buy

I was raised in Louisiana where you grow up learning about many religions, from spirits to voodoo. So when I was a teenager my mother and I made a promise to each other. Whichever one of us died first would leave a sign to let the other know we could be heard after we passed on. Every few years we'd bring it up and renew our promise.

When I married in 1972 I moved to Indiana, into a home that I was told contained spirits. The area had been on an Indian reservation, and there was supposedly an unmarked grave somewhere on the 16-acre property. Objects in the house would move or disappear. My seven-year-old son said people were talking to him, asking him if he liked living there. Visitors who spent the night in a particular room had trouble sleeping. I soon learned it was a good spirit. I figured it just wanted us to know it was there, so I talked to it and all the strange things stopped.

My mother came to visit one summer. She slept in that room, and the next day she said she had felt a presence.

"Were you scared?" I asked.

"Oh, no," she said, "I felt at peace. But remember our promise? If I go first, I'll leave a sign in this area if I can."

Several years later, my mother learned that she had cancer. She was in the hospital 1,000 miles away. I was preparing to pack because I knew her time was near. On the phone she told me that her mother, who had died 12 years earlier, had told her she would be there when the time came. And she told me not to fear, and that she would be there for me when my time came.

After we hung up I told my husband to get ready to leave for the hospital the next morning, and I went to bed early. I woke up at about 8:00 and went into the bathroom. "Good Buy" was written on the mirror. Mom had always spelled "Goodbye" this way because she liked being different. I knew what had happened. Thirty minutes later I got a call from my brother. Mom had passed away in the early morning.

I've never noticed any signs in the years since, but I always feel she's there when I need her, and now I talk to everyone I've lost through the years. Perhaps they do hear us, because since then I've found strength and all of my wishes have come true. I know Mom's there to guide me, and I know she hears me when I talk to her.

—Suzette Wright, Clarksville, Indiana
August 1998

Psychic Dreams and Visions

Approximately one-third of our lives are spent sleeping. Each night we dream, even if we do not always remember our dreams upon waking. Dreams normally help us sort and process the information we receive from each day's experiences. But dreams are also gateways to the subconscious mind. Sometimes dreams and visions, or waking dreams, tap into something larger. Sometimes, for better or for worse, they foretell the future.

A Dream Come True

As I walked the street of the town, I was aware that I had been there before. I didn't know where I was, but I was hungry. I looked for a restaurant.

I walked down a cobblestone hill street. Trolley tracks were visible among the stones. A sign loomed before my eyes: FITZGERALD'S—FINE STEAKS AND SEAFOODS. I stopped in front of a store window that had a large white curtain covering the glass. I opened the door and entered the restaurant. There was a heavy odor of cigar smoke; the smell of beer. A long brown bar with a brass rail extended from the door to the end of the room. Men in coveralls were lined against the stained wood eating beef sandwiches, pickles, and drinking beer. An old-fashioned chandelier hung from the ceiling. I walked to a white-topped table and presently a waitress came through the rear swinging doors to take my order.

As I sat waiting for the food I noticed a stairway inside a nook in the wall. Later, I asked the waitress about the stairway and she said there was a room upstairs for parties.

I left the restaurant and the dream ended.

Another night I again walked the town, down a hill, and into the restaurant. I ordered my oyster soup, and then while waiting for the food I ventured up the rickety stairs to the second floor.

The room was large. A bandstand was at one end and long windows that seemed to rise out of the floor were at the front of the building. Across the street was a gray structure. Below, a trolley climbed the hill with a roar.

Some time later I dreamed again. This time while I was eating my oyster soup someone shouted, "Fire!"

There was a pounding as people dressed in white and black hurtled past me. They came from the room upstairs, down the side stairway and they swarmed into the street. In the summer of 1945 I was a counselor at a co-ed camp not far from Lake George, New York. On my day off I visited the nearby town of Glens Falls. I had never been to that city before and at noontime I sought out a restaurant. A policeman told me to proceed down Glen Street to Fitzgerald's.

As I approached a hill, my knees felt weak; my head felt as though it was encased in cotton. The feeling persisted, and, when the sign came into view, FITZGERALD'S—FINE STEAKS AND SEAFOODS, and the white-curtained window appeared, I felt dizzy.

I walked through the door as "in a dream." A long bar extended through half of the establishment. Men in greasy pants and carrying dinner pails leaned against the brown-stained bar. An old, dusty chandelier hung from the ceiling.

I sat down at a white-topped table and watched the waitress come from the swinging doors in the rear. I ordered oyster soup. Then I saw the stairway in the wall, the gray building across the street.

Pressing my luck I asked the waitress about the upstairs and she said the receptions and dinner parties were held there.

I went upstairs. There was the bandstand at the far end of the empty room. The long windows were in front.

Each day off I came into Glens Falls and ate at Fitzgerald's. I told my friends about the dream and later many accompanied me to the eatery.

In the summer of 1946 I got a job on a farm in Smith Basin, New York. The farmer who hired me was Larry Jenks. He, his wife, and brother Will ran the 350-acre place, 14 miles from Glens Falls.

I told Larry about my experiences there and about my dreams. It was a good topic for conversation. Larry put his fork down and said, "You sit there, Ken." He went upstairs.

He came down carrying a newspaper. Farmers usually save old papers and magazines. He spread the front page before me. The date was July 4, 1946.

I caught a glimpse of the picture showing firemen holding a ladder against a smoky structure. It said briefly, that a fire had struck Fitzgerald's restaurant while a wedding reception was in progress. The guests had escaped injury by using a staircase within the building. The men were dressed in tails and the women in white gowns.

Larry was amazed. I was numbed. Larry asked me for the whole story. I told about the hill, the windows, and the trolley tracks.

"There were trolley tracks, Ken," Larry said gasping. "We tore them up for war scrap."

—Ken R. Schultz, Greensboro, North Carolina
July 1949

Forecast That Came True

It began on July 25, 1945. I was partially awakened by the droning sound of my husband's electric shaver and on the borderline between sleep and wakefulness. Suddenly I saw psychically in boxcar letters out in space these words: "THE WAR WITH JAPAN WILL END AUGUST 4."

That was the way I saw it but I sensed a voice saying, "the 14th." I looked but I could not see the number "1."

When I arrived at my office that morning, before pulling off my hat I said: "Well, put this down in your diaries. Last night I had that same dream and this time I saw the figure "14" as clearly as I see you people standing before me."

I seemed to have an inner knowledge that there was more to it than merely a dream. I wrote a number of personal letters to friends and relatives mentioning my dream. So I had my prediction on record.

On August 10 came word that Japan had asked for surrender terms and on August 14, while we waited with bated breaths for the news that Japan had accepted our terms, one of the personnel, the wife of a soldier, came in from lunch with tears in her eyes, explaining that Japan had refused our surrender terms.

Instantly I said, "But that isn't true." Then I wondered what made me so sure and I realized that in a flash my inner consciousness had seen President Truman standing before the microphone and sensed his saying, "Japan has accepted our surrender terms. The war is over." He did not actually do this until evening.

Following the surrender, my coworkers said, "Are you sure you did not have inside information?" In retrospect I am convinced I did have "inside" information but it did not come from man-made channels.

—Mrs. Katherine W. Price, Washington, D.C.
November 1949

Astral Meeting

In 1909 my wife and I operated a small store in Milwaukee, Wisconsin. My wife's uncle, George Morrison, who also operated a store a few blocks away, was taken ill. He became worse and finally Aunt Zaidie had the attending physician call in a council of doctors.

This council, after a careful examination, gave Uncle George no more than three days to live. On the evening of January 1, 1910, I went to bid him goodbye, for it had been arranged to take him to the home of one of his daughters who lived in Wonewoc, Wisconsin. Aunt Zaidie feared that he would not live to reach Wonewoc.

When I returned home from my visit to Uncle George I went to bed and concentrated on contacting someone on the astral plane who could tell me whether or not Uncle George would live to make the trip.

Shortly after falling asleep I seemed to be led or directed toward a door. Pushing the door open, I entered a large, well-furnished room in which a sandy-haired, ruddy-faced man sat on a couch.

He smiled at me and said, "You came to see me about your uncle, didn't you?" I said I had and he continued, "Your uncle will pass out of physical life on April 17." I thanked him and left.

In the morning I recalled the visit vividly but thought it might have been a dream.

April 17 seemed a long time in the future when a council of learned doctors had given Uncle George only three days to live. The difference was approximately 107 days.

I telephoned Aunt Zaidie and told her not to worry. I told her Uncle George would not pass away until April 17 and explained why I thought so. She called this nonsense and hung up on me.

A few days later I had a violent toothache and being a comparative stranger to Milwaukee I asked one of my customers to direct me to a good dentist. She gave me the name of a Dr. Otto Hoya and I went to see him.

When I opened the door to his office I was amazed to find that he was the man I had met in my dream. He smiled and said, "We have met before, haven't we?" I nodded and he asked, "You came to see me about your uncle, didn't you?"

I said, "Yes, I did."

"And what did I tell you about him?"

"You said he would pass over on April 17."

"That's right," he said and added, "I had forgotten whether it was the 17th or the 7th."

Dr. Hoya and I became close friends and through him I joined the Theosophical Society.

On April 17 Uncle George died.

— G. L. Winsor, St. Louis, Missouri
March 1954

Life Saved by Dream

Back in high school days I was friendly with a local police reporter who did his best to break me into my present profession of columnist and police reporter. One afternoon Bert met me with a big smile.

"Ross," he said, "tomorrow night I'm going to a girl's birthday party. How about coming along; she won't mind." I accepted the invitation.

I retired early and soon fell asleep. I dreamed I was walking down a country lane when I came upon a cottage encircled by a fence, and at the same time seemed possessed with a terrible thirst. I knocked on the door. It opened and before me stood my grandfather (who had died six years previously) smiling and motioning me to step in.

"Bu-but," I managed to say, "you are dead." He looked at me with a broad grin. "No," he said. "I live, but there is something I want to show you." I stepped in.

My deceased grandfather pulled aside two large curtains.

"Look," he said, "don't go to that party with him."

I saw two coffins. In one was my friend, Bert; in the other, myself.

I awoke with sweat rolling down my face and I stayed awake until dawn thinking about my strange dream. In the morning I told several friends including our local city editor.

"Better not go," my priest told me along with a few others who listened.

I phoned Bert and told him about the dream. He laughed the matter aside. I didn't go.

That night Bert's car was struck by a truck. He was killed.

—*Raymond J. Ross, Bridgeport, Connecticut*
January 1950

The Turkish Room

About two or three times a year for 15 years I dreamed the same dream, each time unchanged in any detail. I would enter an unfamiliar room in which walls, ceiling, and floor were covered with Oriental rugs. In the room was a low couch draped with Oriental cloth of the river-loop design. On a small table stood one of those five-by-six-inch calendars that show only the date and the month in large type. Always I noted the date showing on the calendar was May 11.

The dream, recurring so often, became fixed in my memory and remained a continuing source of wonder. What did it mean? It had no action, nothing to give me a hint of its meaning. Although I rarely dream, the meaning of all other dreams usually is clear to me.

The puzzle finally was cleared up in 1932. I had resigned my job as manager of Hearst's New York *American* and before taking another job I decided to tour the Mediterranean. On learning of my plans, Anne Morrow (the sister of Dwight Morrow, United

States ambassador to Mexico from 1927 to 1930) persuaded me to stop over in Turkey and be her guest at Kiz College of which she was a sponsor. Kiz College is located just north of Istanbul (then called Constantinople) and Miss Morrow had arranged for me to live in a house on the grounds during my three-week stay.

On May 11, 1932, I entered the house for the first time—and found the room of my recurring dream, walls, ceiling, and floor covered with Oriental rugs, the foot-high couch (I learned it was called a sedir) and on a small desk a calendar bearing the large print: "May 11."

How can you explain my dreaming for years of a room in a distant land that I was to enter only by what seemed merest chance?

—Bloor Schleppey, Zionsville, Indiana
July 1970

Bloody Handprints

One morning in early 1963 I awoke filled with apprehension. As my sleep-fogged mind cleared, my dream came back to me. What little I remembered made no sense, but parts of it were frightening. I had dreamed of a blood-spattered room and bloody handprints on the wall. In my dream I had left some of my young children with my neighbor Eva, whom

I had never asked to babysit. I could not recall where I had gone but when I returned my little ones were with another neighbor, Margaret, another woman who had never watched my children. The dream bothered me but since I could make neither head nor tail of it, I soon forgot it.

Some months later in June 1963 my nine-year-old son Steven cut an artery in his wrist when he accidentally thrust his arm through the glass pane in our kitchen door. He bled profusely and my kitchen looked like the scene of a massacre. When I called my neighbor Eva, I left bloodyhand prints on the telephone and wall.

Eva offered to take care of my three other children while I rushed Steven to the doctor. When I returned much later my children were with Margaret. Then I remembered my dream!

I thanked God that my son was all right and that my neighbors were so helpful but I was puzzled. I had dreamed the future! Why? How? If the dream was meant as a warning, why hadn't I been able to recall the important part? Even if I had, could I have prevented the freak accident?

It will always remain a mystery to me, but I now am convinced that "unknown" forces work in our lives if we would only heed them.

—Angelica Hefner, Citrus Heights, California
January 1976

My Soul Mate

A lot of mystical events have happened to me, too many to tell them all, but I would like to share one with you.

It happened during tenth grade. My friends, Diane, Ernesta, Chris, and I were girl talking. Then we started to talk about what Mr. Right would be like. When my turn came, I said he would be tall, have green eyes, be very muscular and cute. He would be getting out of the military, the Marines. I would met him in my senior year and we'd marry that same year, in August. His name would be Theodore or Alexander and he would have a short last name.

As the school years went by, I forgot that day until I met him in my senior year. He was everything I said he would be. We both feel that we have found our soul mate. We're very happy. What's my husband's name? Theodore Alexander Ilo.

—Jaylin M. Ilo, Waianae, Hawaii
June 1993

Psychic From Childhood

As a very young girl, while attending a convent in Philadelphia, I had the realization that I was unlike other children. During a school recess we were playing a game and as I took my partner's hand I said to her, "I am so sorry that your grandmother died." She screamed and ran to Sister Mary who was supervising us and reported what I had said.

Sister Mary ordered me to the classroom and followed me in. "Why did you make such a remark?" she asked.

"I don't know," I answered. "But I do know that her grandmother is dead."

I could see that Sister Mary thought me impertinent. She directed that I write 100 times, "I will never again speak about matters of which I know nothing."

I had just taken pencil and paper from my desk when the Mother Superior entered the room. "Madeline's grandmother is dead," she said. "She passed away shortly before recess. Madeline's father called for her a few moments ago. Go back to your play, child," she said to me kindly, "and don't say anything more to frighten your playmates."

My father, without my knowledge, had talked about me to our priest and, of course, the Mother Superior knew too that I was different from the other children. They agreed it would be better not to encourage me in this difference.

When alone, I saw beautiful spiritual beings and sometimes frightening creatures. I heard music when none was being played. My father, being a doctor and an alienist (he now would be called a psychiatrist), had understanding but my mother usually was shocked at the things I told her. She told me to pray.

Father said, "Never speak about these happenings to anyone but us, for others might not understand."

As the years pass, there are times when I cannot see or hear anything unusual. Then I am unhappy, for some of these beings are my beloved companions. But most of the time I can get messages for people.

In 1924 a friend sent a Mr. Martin, a stranger, to me in the hope that I might receive word for him from his wife, who had died several months before. Mr. Martin was grief-stricken. "Why did she have to die?' he asked repeatedly.

"Your wife is still living, Mr. Martin," I consoled him. "She is merely in a different kind of life."

We sat quietly for a little while, then suddenly I saw her and described her to him. She left as suddenly as she had appeared, in company with an elderly man, whom I also described. She had not spoken.

"That was Margaret, all right; you described her perfectly," Mr. Martin said. "Also her father. But why didn't she speak? Doesn't she know how much I miss her?" Before I could reply, he went on, "Maybe you saw her through my mind; you could be a mind reader."

"That is true," I agreed. "I very easily could have seen her through your mind if you were composed. I could have known that you loved to see her comb and braid her long hair each night." He looked startled. "However," I went on, "I could receive nothing from your subconscious mind now, because you are in a state of confusion. If your wife appears again, I will call you."

About three weeks later, a few days before Easter, I was alone in my study. The glow of the sunset was fading and I was about to turn on a light when I felt a presence near me.

"I am Margaret Martin," a lovely voice said. But Mrs. Martin did not appear.

I took pencil and paper and waited.

"There must be something you want to tell me," I suggested.

"Yes, there is," she replied. She then gave me six or seven lines of poetry. They were about Easter, but they seemed not to make a finished piece.

"Tell my husband," she directed, "to look in the middle dresser drawer. In there he will find my notebook. Also give him the paper you have written."

I called Mr. Martin, and shortly afterward he came over. "I didn't know Margaret had this book," he said, handing me a notebook filled with verses.

As we turned the pages we found an unfinished poem about Easter and the lines she had dictated to me made a perfect ending. We were greatly impressed as we now read the completed poem.

"Did I receive this from your mind, Mr. Martin?" I asked.

"Positively not!" he almost shouted. "I never even knew that Margaret wrote poetry."

About a year later he called on me to say he was leaving for the East shortly. I informed him: "You will arrive in Chicago in pouring rain. I see you walking down the street with a large umbrella. As you stop before a bank and begin folding the umbrella, you accidentally brush a woman who also is holding an umbrella. You both apologize and together you enter the bank where she is employed. You meet her again in transacting your business. This is the woman you will marry. You will bring her out here to California to live, and you will have many happy years together."

This all happened as I had predicted. I heard Mr. Martin and his second wife tell the story several times before we drew apart.

—Anna Robeson, Indio, California
June 1960

It Was Our Move!

It happened in Chicago, Illinois, on Christmas Eve, 1927. We had recently come to Chicago and had only our personal belongings to move, no furniture.

"Remember now," my father said as we worked at unpacking, "whatever you dream tonight will come true!"

Mother was unpacking a cardboard carton and stacking the contents on a high shelf in the laundry room. She came to a dead stop. "What do you mean, our dreams will come true tonight?" she asked.

"Haven't you ever heard that before?" Dad asked. "It's an old superstition I used to hear my mother talk about. Whenever a person moves, whatever they dream the first night in their new home is supposed to come true."

"Well, I'd like to dream about a lot of money tonight," Mother laughed, "but I'm too tired. I won't dream at all."

She went back to her unpacking and the rooms were quiet for the next half hour or so.

The early morning light was just beginning to show when I awoke with a shrill scream ringing in my ears. I jumped out of bed and ran into the other bedroom. Mother was sitting up, her eyes wide with fear, one hand pressed against her breast as though to stop the too rapid beating of her heart.

Dad was trying to comfort her. He alternately stroked her hair and patted her back.

"Don't worry, dear," he was saying, "it was only a dream. I could kick myself for mentioning that old superstition. It doesn't mean anything. Please try not to think about it anymore."

"Think about what? What happened?" I asked.

"Just a dream. Go back to bed," he said quickly.

"What was the dream?" I persisted.

Mother was the one who finally told me. She had

stopped crying but her voice still caught on an occasional sob and made little hiccuping noises.

"I saw my brother," she said. "He was working, cutting down a huge tree. All of a sudden, without any warning, it fell!" She covered her eyes for a moment before continuing. It fell right on top of him—pinned him to the ground."

She was no longer speaking to me; she was reliving her dream. "I saw him carried away," she continued. "They took him to a little log cabin on the edge of the woods. I can still see the cot they laid him on." A sob escaped her lips. "They called for a doctor but it was too late. All he did was shake his head and leave."

Father and I spent the next hour trying to convince Mother that she had had only an unpleasant nightmare. We all felt better when the sun finally came up.

It was several hours later when the doorbell rang. Mother was herself again when she walked to the door and opened it. Outside stood a uniformed messenger with a yellow envelope in his hand.

One look at the telegram confirmed our fears. Mother had been right. Her dream had been true. Her brother, Anders Bloom, had been killed by a falling tree early that morning at a lumber camp in Sand Point, Idaho.

Later, when we knew the details of the accident,

we found they coincided exactly with the details in Mother's dream.

Whether it was telepathy, clairvoyance, or merely coincidence, I do not know. But of one thing I am certain—I dread moving!

—Agnes Wendt Guilfoyle, Ontario, California
August 1960

The Blood Ran Red

The blood ran red; it was easy to see from a few feet away. My friend Jennifer Hogue had fallen from her bucking horse onto an upright pipe which pierced her abdomen. Someone helped the girl to her feet and she struggled toward the house behind the horse ring. A few minutes later a small crowd gathered around a vehicle of some sort while Jennifer was eased inside.

This was the dream I described to my mother, Bonnie Rowland, and we both laughed at the violence in my unconscious mind and the way the dream treated Jennifer. I told Mother it wasn't an ordinary dream where everything seems out of sync. I felt the crunch of dirt under my feet and the railing I leaned against was cool. I watched the accident passively and no one seemed to notice me. Except for the accident the dream reflected my everyday life during the time two years earlier when I had kept my mare at Jennifer's stable in Valinda, California.

I had the dream in the summer of 1978 and about four months later my parents were on vacation and my sister Eve and I were home alone. She came home from school one day and told me she met a boy who knew Jennifer. He told her she had had an accident with her horse and described the exact scene I had witnessed in my dream. Her horse threw her, a pipe cut her, and she lost a lot of blood.

—Heather Rowland, West Covina, California
November 1982

To Catch a Thief

Some 20 years ago in Chicago my new husband and I bought an old two-story house, converted it into single rooms, and rented them out to elderly bachelors and widows. We could make a small profit doing this. Of course, we still held full-time jobs to support ourselves. Bob was a salesman for a chemical company and I was a secretary.

Through an ad we found Betty, a motherly widow, who was willing to rent the rooms for us and keep an eye on the place. She did this in return for a free room.

Her references were good and her small room sparkled soap-and-water clean. She must have been quite poor but there was always a little vase of fresh daisies or roses on her windowsill. We trusted her and counted ourselves fortunate to have found her.

One Monday morning after Betty had been our manager for two or three weeks, Bob and I set off to work with light hearts. Sharing a seat on the bus, we smiled into each other's eyes. "What a jewel," Bob chuckled. "Weren't we fortunate to find someone like Betty?"

I agreed happily and opened my morning paper. Then suddenly, for no reason, my body was seized with a series of spasmodic convulsions; at the same time perspiration broke out on my forehead.

"What's the matter, honey?" asked Bob. "Are you catching cold?"

It was 85 degrees outside. The bus was an old vehicle with all windows wide open to catch any stray summer breeze, but I couldn't stop shivering. I tried to laugh it off. "Rabbit running on my grave maybe," I joked feebly.

Then for some seemingly illogical reason I was filled with a strong urge to get off the bus and return home. A voice within me spoke warningly; it almost seemed to scream, "Go home!"

"Bob, we must go back home immediately," I said.

"What's the matter with you? Did you leave the gas on or something?"

"I can't explain. I just know we've got to go back."

Luckily Bob and I are so close that we never need to explain ourselves to each other. Silently, he took my arm and led me off the bus. We didn't wait for a bus going back; we caught a cab.

While Bob paid the driver in front of the house, I rushed up the stairs. Bob hurried after me digging in his pocket for the key. But there was no need to unlock the door.

Our apartment door stood open and there was Betty, mild-mannered, blue-eyed Betty in her hand-embroidered apron, helping herself to our valuables. She was holding the pendant of carved jade Bob had brought back from the service. It had been one of my wedding presents. At the same time she was busy stuffing my mother's crystal and silver spoons into a pillowcase.

Our eyes clung for a second, hers now almost black with panic. She flung a bundle of cash (my next day's bank deposit) out of her apron pocket and sped out the door, nearly knocking us over. We never saw her again.

I often wonder: From what deep well of paranormal knowledge did the message come that sent me racing home?

—Rae Garfield, Hialeah, Florida
January 1983

I Paint the Future

Every once in a while I get an urge to dash off an oil painting, an urge I cannot ignore. My last paintings have either looked into the future or they have triggered future events. I do not know which.

In the winter of 1973, I painted a picture of a woman who seemed to be in a very thoughtful mood and who was obviously pregnant. As I set the painting on top of my secretary-desk to dry, the thought flashed across my mind that I would learn of a pregnancy in my family. And I did, from a most unexpected source. My daughter-in-law Suzi, whose older son soon will be ready for college and whose younger son is 16 years old, informed me in January 1975 that she was three months pregnant. Well, I said to myself, you can't blame the painting for that.

Several Saturdays ago I put the finishing touches to the painting of a big orange cat. This, too, went up on the secretary-desk to dry and less than five minutes later Yip and Buddy began to bark insistently to let me know there was someone at the door. It was raining relentlessly but a lady collecting for the March of Dimes had not let this deter her. I opened the door to give her some money and an orange cat, drenched and forlorn, came running in. Since then he has taken over our home and gets along beautifully with Yip and Buddy. Reds is a beautiful intelligent cat with a lot of Persian in him. But how strange that he should appear just as my painting of an orange cat was completed!

My younger daughter-in-law Marlene, who has two little boys, one three years and the other six months old, has given me strict orders to desist from painting pregnant women.

"Do a painting of money," she urged.

Tongue in cheek, I did an oil painting of a huge bill and put dollar signs all over the rest of the canvas. I received a check for the manuscript from *FATE* while this painting was still wet. It will be interesting to see what else happens.

—Kitty Kaufman, Philadelphia, Pennsylvania
November 1975

Accident Foreseen

In order to miss the heavy daytime traffic of California's Highway 99 my sister and I waited until late evening before leaving Quincy for Los Angeles.

I had been driving several hours and my sister was dozing on the seat beside me when I saw that we were overtaking a 1937 coupe with very dim taillights.

Without warning everything ahead grew strangely misty and I slowed my car. I thought it was a fog patch and I didn't want to hit the coupe ahead. Oddly the coupe remained clearly outlined against this mist while still seeming to be deep in it.

When we were less than a hundred feet behind it, the coupe suddenly swerved to the right. Leaving the highway at a sharp angle it turned over twice and stopped with its wheels spinning in the air.

I put on my brakes and in that same instant the mist cleared and everything was sharply visible in the bright moonlight.

My sister exclaimed, "What was that!" Her question relieved me but I was still extremely puzzled, for apparently I had just witnessed my first hallucination. Her question assured me that she had seen the same thing. Yet at the moment I applied my brakes the mist cleared and the coupe vanished. We got out of our car and checked on foot but there was no evidence that a car had left the road anywhere in that area.

This apparition kept us wondering and talking for the next hundred miles but we came to no conclusion.

On our return trip several days later we passed the same spot and this time it really was foggy. A tow truck was just preparing to right a 1937 coupe which lay upside down on the west side of the road. Because of the traffic and the fog we did not stop to learn the details.

Some persons say that we saw a wreck that actually occurred miles away. Others say we saw the wreck a week before it really happened. My sister and I still wonder.

—Frank Van Zandt, Greenville, California
February–March 1952

Dreaming Ahead

In 1970 when I transferred to the design section of our engineering department where the daily use of a government car was no longer necessary to the job, I bought an old station wagon for commuting. The gas gauge read a constant zero but this was no great problem since the car traveled 20 miles per gallon of gas and I merely had to remember to fill the tank once a week or every 300 miles. As a reminder I kept a record of odometer readings for each gasoline purchase.

In 30 years and 600,000 miles of driving, gas has run out on me four times and on each occasion I have been able to coast as much as half a mile to a pump. Thus I was well aware both of danger and luck in running out and of my inoperative gas gauge when the following incident occurred.

On September 10, 1975, at 6:10 A.M. I woke from a dream which made me uneasy. I recorded it as follows: "Coasted backward down a long grade in car. Backed around in driveway. Turned on motor to proceed."

About 90 minutes later I started over the forested mountain to work. Halfway up the motor stopped. That steep winding road was no place to be stalled, especially for me because I have heart trouble. I maneuvered the car to the left to leave room for any vehicle which might come roaring around the blind curves, and backed carefully until, with a sigh of relief, I coasted backward up a driveway near the bottom. Incredulously I checked my diary and found the tank had indeed been overdriven.

But the car was not tilted forward. Gingerly I tried the starter and after a few grinds the motor started—something it subsequently had refused to do when the car was tilted backward on the mountain. Breathing a thankful prayer I rolled out of the driveway and, using the motor only to maintain momentum on upgrades, made it two and one half miles to the nearest station.

Until I ran out I had not the slightest consciousness of having forgotten to buy gas. Possibly subconscious memory was the only factor behind my early morning dream with its accompanying uneasiness, but then why did the dream portray details completely new to my experience such as backing a long way downgrade, turning in a driveway from which I could head out forward, and actually being able to start the motor to drive away?

—Clifton J. Noble, Huntington, Massachusetts
January 1978

My Clairvoyant Sister

My youngest sister Martha has always been an enigma to the rest of our family. We first noticed it when she was about seven years of age.

At that time we lived in a small town in Oklahoma,

and my father's oldest sister, Aunt Janie, lived in another town about a hundred miles away.

One day Martha kept pestering the whole family with silly questions about Aunt Janie. Such as: Why didn't Aunt Janie ever come to see us? Why didn't we ever go to Aunt Janie's? Did Aunt Janie ever have any children? Why couldn't she go and stay with Aunt Janie? This went on without a letup for four days. We all grew tired of her constant barrage of questions. Then on the fourth day the questions stopped as suddenly as they had started. On the fifth day my parents received a message that Aunt Janie was very ill—and not expected to live.

They left the farm in the care of us older children and rushed to Aunt Janie's bedside. She died a few hours after they arrived.

After they came home they questioned the child as to why she had talked so much about her aunt. But all the child could say was that she just wanted to see Aunt Janie.

My mother and father were convinced that in some mysterious way Martha had been warned of Aunt Janie's death. And listening to our parents we other children began to realize that for some reason Martha was different from the rest of us.

My oldest brother Isaac had always wanted a horse and saddle. So one bright day Father had been to a sale and came home with a beautiful sorrel mare and saddle for him, and he promptly named the mare

Ribbon. Then during the great flu epidemic of the early 1920s my brother got on his horse to go about 15 miles away to work. For some reason Martha started crying and begging him not to go. But he went and all the time he was gone the child cried and worried mother to distraction.

When night came and brother still hadn't come, Dad and Mother both were worried and walking the floor. No amount of coaxing could get Martha to go to bed. The child stood with her little nose glued to the windowpane, staring out into the black night.

Then sobbing she ran to Dad and said, "Ribbon is bringing him home." But it was fully 40 minutes more before we heard a snorting and pawing at the front porch.

Ribbon had brought our brother home, tied in the saddle. Father carried him in and it was many days before our brother was able to tell us that he tied himself in the saddle. After having passed out once he knew he would pass out again so he tied himself in the saddle, headed Ribbon for home and gave her free rein. She brought him straight to the door.

Even to this day when Martha has anyone on her mind for any length of time for no apparent reason we just wait, for we know we will hear from them or of them. Sometimes it's only a letter; sometimes the person she is thinking of will pop in for a visit with us, other times it's news of the person carried by someone else.

One night Martha awoke crying. She said she had seen a man who looked a lot like father standing in long white underwear with his arms crossed on his chest staring at her from the foot of the bed. My father calmly looked at the clock and said it was just 12 o'clock—I wonder what has happened now. He didn't have too long to wait, for a few hours later a long distance call from Ardmore, Oklahoma, told him that his brother was shot in the back at midnight and was dying in a hospital at Sherman, Texas.

Some years later we were visiting another aunt in Arizona when one gray rainy dawn Martha and my aunt were looking out the window. Down the highway from Phoenix and going in the direction of Wickenburg came screaming police cars, motorcycles, and several ambulances.

My aunt said, "Oh my Lord, I wonder what on earth has happened?" To our amazement Martha said, "The Greyhound bus has wrecked up near Wittman, where they have been working on the road. The storm put out the danger flares. All on the bus were killed or injured. One man with both legs and one arm broke crawled a mile to summon help."

We never doubted her. It was another hour before radio station KTAR came on the air with word-for-word news of the tragedy, exactly as she had told it to us.

Down through the years Martha has foreseen every death or accident in our family. The how or why of it we do not understand, but when any one person gets in Martha's mind and she can't get them out, we just wait, wonder, hope, and pray for the best.

—Mrs. Paul Johnson, Brunswick, Colorado
July–August 1952

A Reenacted Crime

I was staying the night with the Damron family in a neighboring town. The Damrons had one room in the old part of the house that they used as a front room or parlor and in which I was to sleep alone.

This front room was almost entirely away from their other rooms. There were three steps leading up to it from a small hallway that led to the front outside door. Across the hall three more steps led down into their kitchen and dining room, with their sleeping rooms above those two rooms.

The front room itself was very long and narrow with only one window. There were, or had been, two doors into this room, the one I have already spoken of and another at the back of the room leading into a long hallway. This door was locked on the inside and boarded up on the hall side. Mrs. Damron had placed her piano at that end of the room and a picture hung above it, so the door did not show.

I did not know there ever had been a door there until the next morning when I told the Damrons my strange dream.

I had barely closed my eyes that night when things began to happen.

The door at the end of the room opened, the piano and other furniture stood against a side wall, and several large men, lumberjacks, sailors, and gamblers, entered.

The room was brightly lighted with lanterns hanging from the ceiling and bracket lamps on a side wall.

The men sat down at numerous small tables and started playing cards. The air was soon thick with tobacco smoke.

At intervals, brightly dressed dance hall girls would come in and sit on their laps, smoke and sip their drinks, then go out again.

Then suddenly the door burst open and a young Spanish boy came into the room. He looked so young, not more than 20, dressed as a pirate, with a wide red silk sash tied around his waist. He had been drinking, and went staggering around the room till he came at last to the couch where I lay, and sat down on the edge of it. He ran his hand over me, outside of the quilt. I lay perfectly still and just looked at him. He was really handsome.

Then all at once one of the big men who had come in first angrily pushed his table away from him, upset his partners, spilled the gold and glasses with a big clatter, and rose to his feet.

He stalked over to the boy on the couch, grabbed the front of his blouse, pulled him to his feet, snatched a large knife from his belt and thrust it into the breast of the boy, then dropped him.

The young Spanish boy screamed once as he fell in a heap on the carpet in front of the couch.

I was terribly frightened but still could not move. I hardly knew if I were awake or dreaming.

Just when I felt I could not possibly stand it another moment, the door in the back opened again. The big man picked up the Spanish boy by the collar and dragged him out of the room. Then everyone picked up their things and trailed after him. The lights went out and the door shut.

I must have lost consciousness or fell asleep for a while. The next thing I remember it was getting daylight.

I looked around the room. It was just as it had been when I had lain down to sleep.

I told my dream to the Damrons at breakfast.

"Why, I call that a wonderful psychic phenomenon," drawled Mr. Damron.

"What do you mean, Mr. Damron?" I asked.

He motioned to his wife.

"I'll tell you," said Mrs. Damron. "That large front room of ours belongs to the old part of this house. It used to be used as a gambling room, oh, long, long ago, and the door that is now boarded up led into a bar and rooms to rent out with women.

"A young boy was murdered in that room many years ago and no one ever learned who did it. His body was found in the alley back of this house."

I shuddered. "I wish I hadn't seen it," I said. "I'll never stay in that room again alone for all the money anyone would give me."

"That's a very strange thing," mused Mr. Damron, "I expect that's about the way it happened."

—Emiline Patterson Hubert, Huntington, West Virginia
April 1951

Premonitions of Death

Death is life's greatest mystery. The death of a loved one often leaves many questions unanswered, many things left unsaid. Sometimes we are prepared for an impending death—warned before it actually happens. A person may receive a warning that seems to help them or someone they know escape an untimely death. In other cases there seems to be nothing that the person receiving the warning can do to prevent it. The following stories tell of such premonitions.

Rehearsal for Disaster

Is it possible for people to foretell the future, even predict the manner of their death? When I was six years old I had an experience that makes me vote yes.

Our family lived in a small town in north Alabama. One of our neighbors, the Cornetts, had a beautiful daughter named Frances, about seven years old, who was noted for her lovely long yellow curls and cheerful disposition. One spring afternoon we children were playing "house." Then Frances suggested we play "funeral."

"Let's pretend that I am sent to town by my mother to tell father to bring some groceries home for supper. As I am crossing the road, Mr. Thompson (superintendent of the local cotton mill) comes along in his limousine. His chauffeur doesn't see me in time and the car strikes me and kills me. Then you all can come to my funeral and mourn for me," Frances said.

She had her way as usual and we played "funeral" as she wanted us to. That very afternoon, exactly as we had "played," she was struck and killed by the identical automobile in the exact manner Frances had described. The next day her little "mourners" attended her real funeral.

—Spears Asherfeld, Pasadena, California
April 1951

The Cross of Light

In our apartment house in the Bronx the neighbor across the hall was a Mrs. Stevenson. One day in 1925, very agitated, she knocked on our door and asked if we would come to her apartment so she could show us something. This was rather unusual, for we weren't that chummy.

Mother and I followed her into her apartment and she led us to her bedroom.

"Look," she said. "Do you see that cross on the wall?"

We were startled by the sight. A large cross of light, its bands a foot or more in width, spanned the whole wall from side to side and from floor to ceiling.

"It has been here for two days," Mrs. Stevenson said. "We don't know what it means or how it got here and we want everyone to see it. Then we'll know it isn't just something we're imagining."

All the people in the apartment house were invited to see the cross of light. The men gathered in the room to try to discover a possible natural cause. They removed all the furniture from the room but the cross of light was still there. Then they covered every possible source of light, every possible chink and cranny, and sealed the door edges from the inside. The great cross of glowing light remained.

Mrs. Stevenson had to contend with a constant stream of visitors when word got around the neighborhood and everyone wanted to see the marvel. It remained on the bedroom wall for a whole week and disappeared when Mrs. Stevenson received word her mother had died. Everyone believed the cross somehow heralded her mother's approaching death.

—Jane Dell, Yonkers, New York
January 1969

A Child's Warning

When I was less than five, we lived in Europe on a large estate. I was playing with my dolls on the lawn when I saw a lady coming up the driveway. She was dressed in very old-fashioned clothes and carried a long-handled parasol with a big ribbon-bow on the handle. My father was a little distance away at the coachhouse speaking to the coachman about the dogs while my mother was in the house.

I ran over to her and dropped a curtsy. She began speaking to me, "I am your Aunt Linda—your father's sister. I have come to tell your father that on the seventh of October his mother will die. If he wishes to see her alive, he must hurry over to America. She is your Grandmother."

I said, "Wait here, I will call Papa!" Running to the coachhouse, I told my father what the lady had said. My father hesitated in coming but I took his hand and pulled him over to the lady who stood waiting on the footwalk. He stood in front of Aunt Linda as I repeated what she had told me about Grandma.

I had never heard of death and I asked the meaning of the word "die." But when I turned toward the lady, I saw she was gone and my father had not spoken a word. He went into the house and dispatched a servant to make steamer reservations for America. We arrived in New York a few days before the seventh of October, on which day my Grandmother did die just as Aunt Linda had foretold on the lawn.

Years later, my father related the following facts to me. That same evening that the lady appeared, he went to the attic, took from a trunk an old-fashioned album, sat me on his lap, and turned the pages of the album slowly. He would say to me, "I bet you do not know who this is!" Suddenly, I recognized a picture and in glee I said, "I do so know who this is! It's Aunt Linda, your sister, who came today to see you!"

This was proof enough for my father. He also told me that my Aunt Linda had died five years before I was born, that she was his favorite sister, that he had never mentioned her name to me nor had he ever spoken of her in my presence!

—Rev. Florence Conners, St. Petersburg, Florida
March 1950

The Clock Mystery

Shortly after we were married, an old bachelor brother and spinster sister asked us if we would live in their home as caretakers while they were away for the winter. We were happy to do so. It was a beautiful old house with grand old furniture. Their hobby was collecting clocks.

On the stairway was an old grandfather clock; over the fireplace was a black ebony with a carved black tiger, and on each side of the piano was a beautiful china clock with Dresden dancing girls on the side. On the old highboy dresser was a gold satin mantel clock and in their dining room a big round wall clock.

When they left they instructed us to keep the clocks wound and running while they were gone. On the morning of April 15 when I arose I looked at the gold clock in the bedroom. It had stopped at 3:15. I knew I had wound it the day before so I looked at the other four clocks.

Every one had stopped at 3:15!

I was mystified and frightened. Our own clock was ticking away as usual. About a half hour later a knock came at the door. When I opened it there stood the old folks' nephew saying that he had just received a telegram that Aunt Lesh had died at 3:15!

—Mrs. Lillian Maxwell, Waukesha, Wisconsin
April 1951

For His Own

When the telephone rang shrilly a few minutes after midnight on April 30, 1969, I was awake and reading in bed. My fourteen-year-old son Charles was asleep in the room next to mine and I jumped up quickly to answer the phone lest it awaken him and my husband Clarence. When I spoke into the phone no one was on the line. Not even a hum could be heard.

As I replaced the receiver I was looking toward the kitchen and all at once there appeared a dark shadow of a large stooped man slowly walking toward me. First I called softly to my husband but he didn't hear me. Overcome with fear I screamed. Clarence rushed into the living room but when I said, "Look! It's going into Charles' room!" he said he could see nothing.

Then Charles called out, "Mother, don't scare me like that. The telephone woke me up too."

Soon I calmed down and we all went back to bed. My husband fell asleep but I lay awake and thought of my oldest sister, Florence Lambert, who lives alone in Man, West Virginia. I thought this might have been a warning that she was ill—but never did I dream this "thing" had come for my only son.

That Wednesday evening, April 30, at about 6:30 I heard Charles crying. When I ran into his bedroom I found him sitting on his bed.

"Mother," he said, "I can't lift my feet from the floor. I am dead up to my waist!"

We rushed him to the Man Appalachian Regional Hospital where I was permitted to go with him to his room. I helped him get into bed and he asked me to pull his legs straight. Then he talked calmly for a few minutes before saying, "Good night, Mommy. Tell Daddy good night for me."

He then seemed to go to sleep—but he had fallen into a coma from which he never awoke. Three doctors worked over him using oxygen equipment but he slept on until about 1:30 P.M. on Thursday when they rushed him to St. Mary's Hospital in Huntington, West Virginia. He died about five minutes after arriving there. The autopsy showed brain fever and traces of lobar pneumonia.

After his funeral on May 4 we came home brokenhearted to an empty cold house. That night we couldn't sleep so my husband and I began to go through his things. We found a letter he had written dated Monday, April 28, two days before he was taken ill. Here is part of his letter:

"Dear Mom and Dad, I love you very much but I just can't go on. Don't worry because God has taken me for his own...."

We had no warning that Charles was going to be taken from us but God had revealed it to him in some mysterious way, then gave us two more days with our only child before he "took him for his own."

—Edna M. Warne, Lyburn, West Virginia
June 1970

The Black Dog

How well I remember the low eerie howl of that little black dog as he pressed his body hard against our front door!

Mama opened the door a crack and tried to prod the dog away with a fire poker, but he would not budge. He just kept up that long, low howl. We knew how upset Mama was when, unmindful of us children, she turned to Grandmother and said, “Someone is going to die.”

Grandma didn’t try to pooh-pooh what Mama said because she knew too that the howl of a black dog meant death. But what no one knew was that the finger of death was pointed at poor Grandma Schroeder. She died a week later from a stroke.

I never forgot that experience. As I grew up and had a family of my own, I never saw a black dog without remembering that eerie keening howl.

After David Evans and I were married I developed a deep and beautiful friendship with a lovely person named Kate. Our lives and ideals were so similar that we seemed more like sisters than just good friends. But as fate would have it, we moved to the South after we retired and Kate and I had to continue our friendship by way of lengthy phone calls and letters.

When my husband died suddenly, Kate was the one who consoled me, often running up huge telephone bills just talking and trying to help me get over the initial shock.

We buried David in a centuries-old cemetery where giant trees, laden with Spanish moss, spread their huge crooked branches in a protective roof over the ancient headstones.

One particularly lovely autumn day my daughter Elizabeth and I went out to the cemetery to put fresh flowers on David's grave. We wandered from one old tree to another, admiring their unusual shapes, when suddenly I felt a presence. Turning, I found a little black dog standing at my heels. He seemed to have come out of nowhere. There were no houses nearby, nor were there other cars or people.

A cold paralysis crept over me and I stood there mute, my mind going back to my childhood and the black dog at Mama's front door.

Not wanting to mention my fear to my daughter, I said nothing about the dog. In what I hoped was a normal voice I said, "Let's go to another part of the cemetery and look at the old headstones." I wasn't really ready to go back home. We got into the car and I thought, thank goodness he didn't howl. But I was still uneasy as I took what I thought was a last look at the little animal.

We drove to another part of the cemetery, a good distance away, and got out of the car to read the headstones. And there again, just a few feet from me, was the same little black dog. I'll never know how he got there in such a short time. I was sure he hadn't followed us as I had looked in the rearview mirror as we drove along and had not seen him.

The little creature dogged my footsteps as we walked around. Finally I couldn't stand it any longer and said to Elizabeth, "Let's get out of here; this dog gives me the willies."

As we headed for the car the dog ran to a headstone, huddled up against it, and let out a long, low howl. I prayed, "Oh, God, not again." But the dog kept up the same low howling as we hurried toward the car. As I passed the dog my eye caught one word on the tombstone—John.

I trembled all the way home, at the same time trying to convince myself that I was allowing myself to be upset by an old wives' tale.

After a light Sunday night supper we watched television and then went to bed. I felt better the next morning and gradually over the next few days the experience faded into just another memory.

About two weeks later, I received a letter from Kate:

"Dearest Anne," she wrote. "I couldn't call you without breaking down...." As I read those words a piece of paper fell to the floor. I stooped to pick it up and found it was a picture of Kate's husband Johnnie, with these words above it: "Funeral Services for Johnnie E. S——."

He had died on my birthday, November 2, 1976.

My thoughts raced back to the headstone with its name John and the little black dog that had huddled against it, howling its news of death.

—Anne Evans, Savannah, Georgia
March 1980

A Cheap Gray Coffin

In 1932, during the time when Benito Mussolini and his Fascist regime dominated Italy, my father Michelino Toia decided to journey there to sell the home and several acres of land that he had inherited from his parents some years before. We all agreed that since none of us intended ever to live in Italy, it would be better to buy a home here in the United States with the proceeds of the sale. My father had been a naturalized American citizen for more than 35 years.

When Father had been gone only three days, at approximately 6:00 A.M. on a Tuesday morning I got out of bed and as usual opened the kitchen door to see what the weather was like. My husband would be leaving for work at 7:00.

To my horror I was confronted with a most terrifying apparition. Lying horizontally against the inside of our fence, about 15 feet from the house, was a cheap gray wooden casket. It was open and my father lay dead inside it. This was not a dream. I actually saw this.

The apparition lasted for only a moment because I instantly shut the door. I was so terrified that I couldn't even scream.

I did not tell my husband about this terrifying thing before he went to work but I did tell him that evening when he came home. He had by now become interested and puzzled by my many strange experiences and advised me not to tell my mother or the rest of the family about it—not yet anyhow. He said something might happen to prevent what I had seen from happening and my father would not really die. At this time Father was still on the ship en route to his destination.

I took my husband's advice and tried to dismiss the incident from my mind. But try as I might I kept visualizing my father lying dead in that cheap coffin. The following day, just a few minutes before awakening in the morning, I dreamed I was at my sister's house. She and her husband lived about two blocks away from us. And I was holding a letter in my hands and reading it to her. We both began to cry. Now I knew I should no longer keep from my mother and the rest of the family what I felt certain would become a reality.

The uncanny thing about my second dream was that the letter that I was reading to my sister gave complete and detailed information as to how, when, where, and why my father was to meet his tragic end. The name of the town where Father was to have his fatal mishap seemed to stand out boldly. I was born in Brooklyn, New York and never have been to Italy. I did not know the names of Italian towns, their locations, or distances from the house of my father's parents, except for the name "Gezzeria" in the province of Catanzaro in Calabria where Father had told us he was born.

The dream letter was written in very black ink, in characteristic European script, on a single folded sheet of paper. It read in part: "Your father is going to be killed. He overslept his hometown station-stop and was forced to get off at Reggio. He is a stranger there and all alone."

I kept repeating "He is going to be killed . . . he is going to be killed . . . he is a stranger there and all alone" and crying uncontrollably in my sleep as I read the letter to my sister. This terrifying dream woke me. My face was wet with tears and I was trembling. I knew this was no ordinary dream.

That night when my husband came from work I told him my second dream and he agreed that I should tell my mother and the rest of the family about my two strange dream experiences.

My family just stared at me. My two brothers pretended to joke about it. One of them said, "Why don't you try to dream something pleasant once in a while?" But I could tell that he, like the rest of us, felt anxious and uneasy.

Our worst fears were confirmed by a letter we received from the American Consul less than a week later. It told us that Father had overslept his hometown station-stop and been forced to get off at the next stop, Reggio in Calabria. There he was picked up by two Fascist soldiers who, after a lengthy interrogation, accused him of being an American spy—something that God and all the saints in heaven know my poor father never was.

During the course of the interrogation my father became angry and kept repeating, "I'm only an American tourist. I am only an American tourist. I am very tired. I am 60 years old. Please leave me alone." This apparently infuriated the soldiers and they began to struggle with him. The American Consul went on to explain, "Michelino Toia accidentally fell out of a second story window, to his death. And since there was no one there to claim his body he has been buried in a pauper's grave." That explained the cheap gray wooden casket!

But the letter I had read in my dream was not the American Consul's, but one which arrived a few weeks later from an aunt, Mrs. Clara Ianni of Gezzeria. Her letter, on a single folded sheet of paper, written in very black ink and the characteristic curling European script, gave us all the detailed information that had been in my dream letter.

—Rose E. Melaro, Silver Spring, Maryland
January 1976

A Still Small Voice

During the first year of World War II my husband Charles had to leave his work at Camp Hood (now Fort Hood, Texas) and return to our home in Houston, Texas. He was desperately ill. The doctor's examination revealed gallstones. He administered an emergency injection to stop the intense pain, then advised immediate surgery.

My husband had a horror of surgery and said he would never submit to an operation. The doctor told me it was the only hope. I was torn between my husband's fear and the doctor's grave warning. I yearned to plead with him to follow the doctor's advice but I compelled myself to silence. It was Chuck's decision, not mine.

Thus it happened that on a July day in 1942 we sat in the car outside the hospital waiting for him to make up his mind. He finally broke down and wept, saying he would submit to the operation if I would make arrangements for his admittance. Since he was so desperately ill, I immediately started up the stairs to the hospital entrance. In my mind I heard that still small voice: "You're making his funeral arrangements."

I stopped dead still and almost collapsed. I prayed, "Lord, what shall I do?" Then the doctor's grave warning rang in my ears. Charles' only hope lay in the immediacy of the operation. I went on to make the necessary arrangements and soon Charles was in his hospital bed. The doctor came, all smiles, assuring my husband he had made the right decision. I felt like Judas. I couldn't tell anyone about the voice.

From then on everything seemed to work by divine pattern. Charles' youngest sister came from California, knowing nothing of his hospitalization. This caused him great anxiety but he seemed to accept her arrival more passively when we assured him she had not been summoned.

The operation proved successful. He suffered not at all and in nine days of convalescence he enjoyed company and maintained a cheerful mood. But on the ninth day he took a drastic turn for the worse and on July 23, 1942, he died—suddenly and unexpectedly. I hated myself for not listening to the small voice.

After the funeral, however, events proved that he was destined to die. My son David, then only 15, had never driven a car without company—but to get to the bedside of his ill father he had to drive alone a distance of 200 miles. He told me a woman draped in white sped before the car all the way home. He took this as a forewarning. My sister-in-law's unexpected return, my husband's final submission to the operation and my own warning all added up. But the compelling incident occurred when we were going through the contents of Charles' billfold. He had the July page of a small calendar neatly folded and tucked into one of the small pockets. The 23rd—the day of his death—was completely blacked out.

Only then did I remember my husband's intuitive gift. He told me that whenever he met anyone a date instantly flashed into his mind. For a long time he didn't realize these dates had any significance but as he grew into maturity he began to pay more attention. He confessed to me that he became very depressed when he realized the dates were specifically that person's day of death. At that time I chided him and wouldn't take him seriously.

This memory brought a realization that filled me with deep remorse. I learned never to take a God-given gift lightly. I regret that I could not heed the warning of that still small voice but I have a loving memory of my husband, knowing how bravely he went to the hospital and submitted to the operation—one he knew he would not survive.

—Della E. Nugent, Houston, Texas
March 1969

Broken Promise

The afternoon of July 28, 1927, was perfect for our promised boat ride on *The Favorite*, a double-decker boat making short excursions on Lake Michigan between Chicago's Municipal Pier and Lincoln Park.

My six-year-old daughter and my mother had suggested *The Favorite* because its red and white decorations and leisurely cruising would make the outing seem more festive. I promised readily because I feared the small motor boats with their spurts of speed.

When we stepped onto the pier we saw *The Favorite* slowly approaching her dock. The water gleamed blue and green, rippling gently. My daughter urged us to hurry but I explained there was plenty of time. Passengers had to disembark and Captain Arthur Olson wouldn't start off again until there were sufficient passengers to make the trip worthwhile.

As we walked eastward a boatman invited us to board his motor launch for a ride to the park.

"Thank you," I said, "we're taking *The Favorite.*"

A bit further another boatman extended an invitation. My little girl exclaimed, "We're taking the big boat."

"Good!" he answered, "you'll enjoy it. She's a beauty."

As we went on, a third boat owner stepped forward saying, "This is your boat for Lincoln Park, ladies."

Without the slightest hesitation I answered, "Yes, this is the boat."

He lifted my youngster into the boat and she screamed, "This isn't the boat! Mother, you promised!"

I motioned my mother to step aboard and her dark eyes sparked anger. I paid our fares and in a few moments we sped away.

I was sorry I had caused disappointment, but not sorry I had broken my promise. When the man said, "This is your boat," I felt a sharp sensation between my eyes and something mysterious assured me that this was the boat for our ride.

Arriving at Lincoln Park my mother insisted I cancel the return trip to the pier. "We'll take the trolley home," she snapped. At home she slammed her bedroom door shut, indicating her displeasure.

I drew my child close to me. "Darling," I murmured, "promises should be kept but this one had to be broken. I don't know why."

She gave me a forgiving kiss.

A little later the streets were electrified with shouts of "Extra! Extra!" from the newsboys. I sent my daughter to the door to buy a paper.

The banner headline on the *Daily News* extra for July 18, 1927, read, "25 Drowned As Lake Boat Sinks." The story stated that *The Favorite* had capsized a half mile off North Avenue in a sudden terrific squall.

What I still do not understand is why and how some mysterious force directed me to break my promise when so many others were doomed to die.

—Blanche Weidmuller, Ft. Lauderdale, Florida
July 1965

Beloved

On March 8, 1983, my mother, Pauline Howell of Lake Grove, New York, awoke to tell me she had dreamed that she was buying a huge bleeding heart inscribed "Beloved—." She couldn't make out whose name followed that word.

My mother was not well. She was suffering from severe diabetes complicated by heart disease.

The next day at 5:45 P.M. Mother was sitting at the kitchen table; I was busy preparing dinner in the kitchen and my daughter was sitting near the back door watching the stray cat we often fed. Suddenly we all heard a single knock at the door.

When my daughter went to see who it was, she found no one there. I went to check for myself. As I was walking toward the door, I noticed that the cat was eating calmly. If anyone had been nearby, the animal, which didn't like people, would have behaved differently.

"Maybe it's the knock of death for me," Mother said. She died the following morning at 6:50.

At the head of her casket was a huge bleeding heart. It was inscribed, "Beloved Mother."

—Laurie Howell, Lake Grove, New York
February 1984

Nightmare Death

One night almost four years ago, in May, 1956, I dreamed my four-year-old cousin, Bobbie Hoch, was playing with a toy gun. Bobbie was at home in Takoma Park, Maryland, and he pointed the gun at himself and said, "Bang! I'm dead." Then he fell on the floor.

I awoke from this dream and started to cry. My mother came to see why I was crying. She asked what had happened. I told her the story of my nightmare.

For the rest of the night I couldn't sleep and I got up early, planning to call my aunt, Mrs. Charles Hoch, to see if my cousin was okay. But it was too early. I knew they would be asleep so I went back to bed for an hour. When I got up again and finished dressing the phone rang. Mother answered it.

I ran downstairs in time to see Mother drop the phone and start to cry. I picked up the dangling receiver to ask what had happened.

My uncle, Charles Hoch, was on the line. He said in a sobbing voice, "My baby boy is dead. I found him on the floor after hearing a gun go off. The ambulance came but he died while going to the hospital."

He then dropped the phone and I could hear him continue to sob. I stood completely still—too shocked to move—but I realized that my dream of the night before was as true as it had been clear.

The horrible thing had really happened.

I keep reproaching myself for not having called the Hoch home sooner. Maybe Bobbie would be alive today.

—G. Helen Morgan, Washington, D.C.
March 1960

Timely Omen

In the mid-1960s my mother Marguerite gave me a watch for my birthday. It always kept good time until she died. Riding home after her funeral on November 21, 1967, I noticed the watch had stopped. I took it to a repair shop twice and each time it ran for a day or so and stopped again. Finally I gave up on it and bought another watch.

In August 1979 my father Harold was stricken with cancer and knew he had only a few months to live. During the last week of his life his watch stopped running and the clock in his room also stopped. Father was a dedicated clock-watcher and insisted that I give him my watch. When I returned to the hospital to see him the next day, Father was angry because my watch had quit on him as well.

This had to be an omen of approaching death, for my watch started to run again when I put it back on my wrist.

But when Father died on December 4, 1979, that watch also quit for good.

—William Wingfield, Covina, California
February 1982

Egyptian Sand Reader

Charlot, the girl I loved, and I had finished dinner at Miss Ann's, one of the quaint candle-lit restaurants that used to exist in Hollywood back in the glamorous 1930s. We came out of the restaurant into a lovely starlit night.

Charlot was in a happy mood and seemed full of laughter. I too felt the happiness of the occasion and the night and said, "Charlot, why not drive over to Sunset Boulevard and see what's going on?"

Charlot said, "Oh, that sounds like fun. You never know what you might find on Sunset."

At that time the Boulevard was not the glamorous place it is today. So I headed the car down the slight incline onto Sunset. Shortly we saw a decrepit frame house bearing a large fading sign which read, "Know Your Future. The Egyptian Sand Reader Will Tell You Your Past, Present, and Future."

I stopped the car and we both stared at the sign. Then Charlot exclaimed, "Oh, wonderful. Let's go in and see what the Sphinx has to tell us!"

The sign appealed to me too, so I parked the car and we entered a rather drab waiting room. Soon a woman, looking as old as time, entered the room. Her face was wrinkled and her body bent from age. Clutching an old shawl covered with mystic markings, she said quietly, "I was expecting you. Come into the other room, please."

We followed her into a strange room with zodiac signs painted on the walls. The room was practically barren except for an eight-by-ten-foot slanted board covered with mystic symbols which appeared to be Egyptian. There were several old cushions at the foot of the board on which to sit and it was not until we all were seated that I saw that the seeress sat near a large box of white desert sand.

The strange woman closed her eyes and muttered some kind of chant. Then she began to pick up one handful of sand at a time and cast it slowly at the board. After a few such throws, she began to tell us things about our pasts, all of which were amazingly true. Then she threw more sand and began to tell us about the future.

Suddenly she stopped and I saw a fleeting look of pain cross her face. Then she said to me, "I would like you to stay in this room but I would like your beautiful young lady to step out into the waiting room."

Charlot laughed merrily, got up and went into the other room.

When the elderly woman and I were alone, she closed her eyes and muttered strange unintelligible words as she cast more sand on the board. When she spoke again it was with a great sadness in her voice. "Within the next year you shall lose the greatest treasure of love a man can ever have."

I looked at her in bewilderment as she continued, "The beautiful young lady with you shall be killed instantaneously. She shall be killed by a speeding truck on a boulevard—it shall be in about six months—around Christmastime, when she is running impetuously across the street to a shop where she has ordered you a special Christmas present; she wants to make sure she can get it for you in time for Christmas.

"The sands of fate are never wrong. It is written in Destiny!"

I got up off the cushion feeling shaken. The old woman said kindly, "There is nothing you can do about it. Just be as kind and loving to her as you can while she is still here."

Somehow, I managed to pay her the pittance she asked and got out. In the waiting room I took Charlot's hand and without a word we left. Charlot sensed my mood had suddenly changed and I had become sad. She didn't say anything but became more cheerful and full of laughter, trying to cheer me up. She thought the visit to the sand reader had been just a lark and paid no attention to it.

But everything the strange seeress had said came true down to the last detail. Charlot did run across a busy boulevard to check on a Christmas present that she wanted to be certain would be finished by Christmas. She was struck by a truck and killed instantly; apparently Destiny is Destiny.

Since then I have had many other loves but none like Charlot. Her memory haunts me to this day. The aged seeress spoke truly when she said, "You shall lose the greatest treasure of love that any man could ever have!"

—Paul M. Vest, Los Angeles, California
May 1982

The Death Angel

Growing up in the country before rural electrification, my friends and I entertained ourselves late into the evenings telling ghost stories and hunting for ghosts. But no matter how hard I tried, all my ghosts turned out to be something real—until I met the Death Angel.

A few years earlier we had moved to central Florida, out in the country of course where the water came from an outside pitcher pump on the west side of the house and the privy was on the east side out a ways. Entering the house you crossed the porch on the north side and went through the bedroom in which my parents and I slept, then into the kitchen where the galvanized water bucket with its enamel dipper sat.

One night in February I awoke feeling terribly thirsty; I must have eaten something salty before retiring. Noticing that the kerosene lamp on the tired old dresser was still burning, I got out of bed and went through the doorway into the kitchen. Reaching for the dipper I quenched my thirst. When I turned back, I saw a tall figure in the glow from the bedroom lamp. Man or woman, I'll never know! It was dressed in a black floor-length cloak, neither loose nor tight-fitting. Its head covering was like a nun's headgear except entirely black, midnight black. Where its face and hands should have been was only blackness—no eyes, no mouth, no nothing. It was as if the cloak and hood were filled with a nonexistent figure.

For a moment I stood aghast, then decided it must be my imagination or a trick of the lighting. Putting it from my mind, I went back through the bedroom and onto the porch on my way to the outside john. As I stepped through the outside door, there the black figure stood again!

I had always wanted to find a ghost and had diligently hunted for one. This seemed to be my chance! I reached out with hand extended to touch the specter; my hand and arm went right through! I could see my arm right through that awful specter. I forgot the john and went back to bed, shivering.

A few days after this, one of my father's lungs collapsed and he died a short time later.

A long time later I told old Annie Bonney, a dear neighbor, what I had seen. I told it hesitantly for fear she would think I was hallucinating.

"No, child," she said, "you were not seeing things. What you saw was the Angel of Death who appears to some people to warn them of the approaching death of someone dear."

Perhaps she was right; my father and I were exceptionally close. But I'll never hunt another ghost.

—Phoebe Cole, Lorida, Florida
June 1982

What's in a Picture?

In 1983, my mother, Mary Dorothy Callahan, and her two sisters, Harriet Young and Verna Dorschied, were visiting Corrine Thielman, my sister, in Seattle, Washington.

One evening all three were snuggled together in a big king-size bed, just as they had when they were all little girls. My sister snapped a picture of them together.

The picture was particularly memorable, so Corrine sent me a copy. There they were—my mother and my two aunts. Of the three, Aunt Verna was the eldest and Aunt Harriet the youngest.

In 1986, when Mom had been back home with me in Las Vegas, she asked if I still had the picture of her in bed with her sisters. Getting the picture out of the album, I was astounded to see that in the one I had with Mom with Aunt Verna, there was just a big space in the middle.

I handed the photo to Mom and she said, "Doesn't Harriet look a little bit yellow here?"

I looked again, and indeed, all three ladies were in the bed. I put the picture back and decided the entire incident was my imagination.

Aunt Harriet and Aunt Verna both lived in Milwaukee, Wisconsin. In November 1986, we received a phone call from Aunt Verna. Aunt Harriet was in the hospital with cancer of the pancreas. Harriet Young died less than two months later.

The next few years were busy for me. I worked at a local radio station, kept my home in order and an eye on my mother, who was now on dialysis due to kidney failure.

One Saturday in October 1989, I was dusting the living room and came across the photo album. I began thumbing through it, more to avoid work than anything, and I came across the page with the photos of Mom's trip to Seattle. There was the picture of the ladies in bed. I let out a scream and burst into tears. There was only one person in the bed—Aunt Verna. When I dried my eyes and looked again, all three ladies were in bed, but somehow I knew.

I called my sister. I knew she would think that I was out of my mind, but I had to tell her that we would lose Mother soon. Corrine was comforting, but she thought that I was being hysterical.

On January 9, 1990, my mother went into a coma, never to awaken again. On January 27, 1990, at 11:10 P.M., my mother, Mary Dorothy Callahan, died at Sunrise Hospital in Las Vegas.

Verna Dorschied, my remaining aunt, lives in her own apartment in Milwaukee. As long as she lives, I will not look at the picture again. I do not want to know. I loved them all too much.

—Mary Anne Callahan Morgan, Avondale, Arizona
April 1993

Death Stood Waiting

It was 1918. The war in Europe was drawing to a close after four long years when a new scourge added its toll to that of World War I. Influenza!

I was a young girl of 12. My cousin Lillian and I had been close friends through childhood as our homes, in Los Angeles, were built one street apart with a large vacant lot separating the two properties. But our hours of playtime together were temporarily abandoned when Lillian's parents contracted the flu.

There was a shortage of doctors and nurses at this time and when my mother found they could only get one nurse for her brother and sister-in-law she volunteered to stay with them and help in any way possible. Then, as in most cases, the house was quarantined to help keep the disease from spreading any further.

I was greatly concerned for my aunt and uncle, lonesome for Lillian, and I missed my mother terribly. Before the quarantine was set Mother and I had agreed to say goodnight by signaling with a flashlight across the vacant lot. At every sundown I patiently awaited the signal that wished me a loving goodnight.

One evening, while waiting for the signal, I noticed a white figure walking back and forth along the fence in my cousin's yard. I didn't pay too much attention and when my mother's signal came I went quietly to bed, always with a prayer that the next day would bring good health to my aunt and uncle and good things would be as before.

The next day, however, showed no signs that my prayers were being answered so, once again, I waited by the window for the small beam of light that allowed me to go to bed in peace. And once again I saw the white figure pacing the yard. Its presence was beginning to bother me when a flickering light from a second-story window distracted my gaze. As I left the window I noticed the figure was gone.

On the third day Lillian's father had improved slightly, but her mother showed no gain.

At dusk I again waited at the window and wondered if the white figure would appear. Suddenly, it was there; only on this night it was clothed in black. As I watched it pacing slowly back and forth across the yard fear crept up my spine. Then the pacing figure stopped and gazed up at a second-story window in my cousin's home. Mother's flashlight shone across the vacant lot and I went to bed.

The next morning I saw my cousin come running across the lot and I ran down to meet her. Suddenly I knew, though no words were spoken, my aunt was dead.

—Wilma Hays Goodcell (as told to Patricia Goodcell Huff), San Bernadino, California October 1964

Her Eyes Live Forever

My wife Premkuvar knew three months before her death when she would be leaving her mortal coil. We had been married very young and lived a happy married life for 60 long years. Premkuvar was religious-minded and pious and when my mother was on her deathbed, she entrusted the worship of our family deity, Lord Krishna, to my wife, saying, "Believe in the God as a living power and not an idol." Premkuvar was so engrossed that she would talk with the idol and Lord Krishna appeared in her dreams.

In 1961 she was struck with paralysis but her willpower was so strong that thereafter she went on four pilgrimages, one to about 9,000 feet above sea level on a Himalayan mountain. She undertook this religious journey of 84 miles, traveling on foot. Rains came during the journey and she had to travel in knee-deep water.

A priest was also traveling with the pilgrims and she spoke to him, saying, "Brother, I am paralytic and it is difficult for me to carry my bag. Please carry it for me."

The priest said, "Mother, I am already carrying the load of other pilgrims. I can carry no more."

"As God will," Premkuvar said.

She was plodding along slowly when another priest came to her and said, "Mother, I will carry your bag."

When she asked his name he said, "My name is Shriji." (Shriji is one of the names of Lord Krishna.) He carried her bag throughout the journey and when she returned she told me, "The Lord came to me in the form of a human being and carried my load."

In 1977 I was afflicted with throat cancer. When I was being taken to the operating theater for surgery, she said, "Do not be afraid. Nothing will happen to you because it is destined that I will go before you."

The intuition that she would die on July 2, 1982, came to her at 11:30 one night in March of that year.

But I did not know that when she said, "I wish to donate my eyes to the eye bank when I die but I have a cataract. I want it to be removed." After it was removed, she put new clothes and beads in the corner of her cupboard and said, "These clothes should be put on my corpse."

In April a Japanese doctor, N. Masuko, came to our house to ask me to take part in a conference of cancer laryngectomees in Tokyo on July 5. When my wife learned that I was to leave on July 2, she told the doctor, "My husband will not be able to fly on July 2." She told me not to accept.

On June 24 a producer, Jayesh Gokani, came to tell me my new play was scheduled to open July 4 at an upcountry center and we would be leaving on July 2. (I am a playwright and film writer.) The same answer came from Premkuvar: "He cannot come on July 2. If you want him, change the date of the premiere showing."

On July 1 our architect-friend Omprakash Sharma came to our house and casually asked, as he did on every visit, "How are you, mother?"

"I am going to God's abode," Premkuvar replied.

The next night at 11 o'clock I was writing when she called. She bowed to me and said, "I am going," and began to chant the name of Lord Krishna. Our son Madhav came running from the adjacent room and she told him, "I am going. Nobody should cry after I leave the body."

Within 10 minutes she was gone.

Her eyes were donated to the eye bank and in the morning we were told that they had been grafted to a blind person. A few days later I told my son, "I wish to see those beloved eyes that loved me for 60 years." But my son said no. He feared I would not be able to control my feelings.

I only wish to tell the person who received Premkuvar's eyes that he should also donate them in the event of his death. My wife is gone but her beloved eyes will live.

—Pragji Dossa, Bombay, India
August 1984

Grampa and St. Bridget

Michael Tomaino, my grandfather, was 84 years old when he passed away. He was a devout Roman Catholic who went to mass every morning before starting a new day. He lived next door to St. Mary of Mount Carmel Church in Utica, New York. He was very close to my grandmother Saveria Tomaino, who passed away on January 28, 1938. My grandfather took her passing much to heart.

Because he was alone and old, my mother requested that Grampa come and live with us, five blocks away from his old apartment. We lived in a two-family house that we rented and had an extra bedroom for Grampa to stay in. We lived on Mary Street, and on the corner was St. Agnes Catholic Church.

Grampa hated to leave his apartment, but he finally consented because there was also a church near our house. My grandfather always told his daughter, Felicia Alberico, my mother, that he prayed all the time to St. Bridget, because she is the saint who lets you know in some form or another when you are going to the Lord.

I was nine years old then, and remember this clearly. It was July 3, 1938, the same year my grandmother died, when my grandfather came home from church after attending mass. He told my mother to prepare herself and get things ready for him because he was going to the Lord within two days.

She told him to stop talking like that because he was in good health and he shouldn't talk about dying. He told my mother that St. Bridget gave him a sign that morning.

After mass he didn't leave the church as usual. Something inside told him to sit there. As he was sitting alone in the empty church, he kept looking over at the lit candles. It was unusual that there were only two candles lit among many unlit ones, since there were always a vast number of lit candles there.

After he had looked at them for a while, one of the candles directly in front of him went out for no apparent reason. There was no stirring of wind, for no one was around; it just extinguished itself.

He knew strongly that it was a sign St. Bridget gave him of his passing, and how many days by the two candles. The next day he was rushed to St. Elizabeth's Hospital, where he died the second day, July 6, 1938. I will never forget it.

—Vera Grzywacz, Utica, New York
April 1993

Out of Body Experiences

There are those who believe that we, as human beings, consist of more than just our physical bodies. We also possess an astral body. This astral body is said to be capable of leaving the physical body to journey across the room or even around the world. Sometimes, while drifting off to sleep, under anesthesia, or after a traumatic injury to the physical body, the astral body leaves the physical body behind. The following stories are personal accounts of this phenomenon.

Tonsils

In July 1941, my parents, Anne and Wilson Hales, decided to have my tonsils taken out. The procedure was scheduled to take place in Doctor Dumenti's treatment room, in Bountiful, Utah.

I remember wearing a nightgown and being told to lie down on the operating table. The nurse then placed a cone over my nose and mouth and poured a sticky, dark substance through the opening. It had a peculiar smell. I was told to breathe deeply.

All at once I was in a red tunnel with silver stars shooting past me and the sound of eerie music that increased as I moved rapidly upward. Suddenly the tunnel vanished and I found myself bumping against the ceiling of the operating room. I turned and looked down.

Below me, I saw myself lying on the narrow table. The nurse stood by a metal tray, handing the doctor steel instruments. I saw my mouth being held open by metal things (a child of eight, I had never seen forceps, clamps, or other surgical apparati. I felt oddly weightless as I watched. The room seemed deep. I had never before been up to the ceiling and it was curious to me that I should be able to see myself lying on the operating table. This lasted some time. Then, everything vanished and I was waking up, crying silently at the pain in my throat. What happened was an out-of-body experience. I have since read about other people to whom this has happened. To me it proves that the soul is a separate entity from the body and that we do survive death.

—Mary J. Seiler, Pahrump, Nevada
October 1993

She Didn't Die Alone

To wake up in a hospital at 3:00 A.M. is about as inspiring as visiting a city morgue. I yanked at the covers and closed my eyes hoping the sleeping pill hadn't given out. But something tugged at my eyelids. I was in Doctor's General in San Jose, California, and my acute bronchial infection seemed to be responding well to treatment. Why couldn't I sleep?

My thoughts turned to the evening before—October 9, 1968—when I telephoned my home in Santa Clara about 7:00 P.M. My husband Chuck said he had everything under control but I sensed a note of anxiety in his voice.

"Yes, there's a little problem," he confessed. "The mare seems to have a bit of colic but I called the vet. He said to keep her on her feet until he gets here. Now don't you worry about her."

But I did worry and two hours later I called a second time. Dr. Hambey had seen the horse and would return at midnight to give her another injection.

The nurse, Mrs. Torkelson, took the phone from

me, cradled it and popped a thermometer into my mouth. A needle stung my bottom. I'd be asleep soon.

Suddenly I was awake. I strained to see my watch. It couldn't be! Yes, it was three o'clock. I wanted to sleep but something kept me from it. I closed my eyes only to have them forced open. As I stared at the ceiling a force seemed to pull at me, sucking like a noiseless vacuum sweeper. I was helpless against it.

Then I found myself looking at my husband, exhausted and asleep. In her stall stood the mare, a four-year-old quarter horse we called "Bobby Sox." Her chocolate-brown eyes seemed calm and her muscles relaxed. I watched her for some time, just as I often sat and studied the horses. Suddenly her flanks heaved and her head dropped as she strained to cough. Her front knees buckled and she went down. She kicked, rolled, and bit at her flanks as if trying to relieve her pain. It wouldn't help. She was bound in the stable now and never would get up. She stopped fighting and lay still.

My private circuit went dead and my eyes closed but I could not sleep. I cried silently for the dead mare. In desperation I called for help. Light flooded the room and Mrs. Wathe, the night nurse, came to me. She gave me another injection and pulled the side rails higher. Now I seemed helpless to keep my eyes open.

In the morning the tears came as I remembered the vision.

"Oh, come now, you can't know that," said Mrs. Wathe. "Cheer up, she'll be fine." She did not believe I had seen the mare die.

I dialed home. Chuck's voice sounded strained. "I left her at 3:00 A.M., calm and in no visible pain. I lay down and fell asleep for about an hour." He hesitated, then said, "I hate to tell you this—"

He didn't have to tell me. I was with the mare when she drew her final breath and settled into lasting sleep.

—Colleen Shull, Santa Clara, California
February 1969

Christmas Journey

I lay on my bed feeling a great longing to be with my family in Sweden. It was Christmas Eve in 1925 and I had been in the United States a little more than a year. I was only 20 years old and had few acquaintances—partly because I knew little English. As I lay thinking about my loved ones my homesickness grew even more intense.

Suddenly it seemed as if I were disembodied, whirling through space and wind and mist, until I found myself at the gate leading to our family home in Sweden. The snow lay deep in the valley and the firs and pines wore mantles of white. I started up the familiar hard-trodden narrow path across the yard, hearing my own crisp footsteps and looking up at the frosted windows.

A voice broke the silence. "You cannot go in." I pleaded to be able just to see my loved ones through the windows. Again the voice spoke. "You cannot speak to them." Through a circle thawed in the hoarfrost on one window I could see my mother, Anna Ekback, looking up at the window and pointing. My brothers, Albin and Alex, were decorating the Christmas tree. I heard them talking as Albin, following my mother's gesture, turned toward the window.

Just then there came a loud knocking on my bedroom door and immediately I was back in my bed in my Chicago apartment. My landlady, Mrs. Gunnil Nelson, stood in the doorway. When I tried to speak I found I was having difficulty breathing; I had a terrible pain in the region of my diaphragm. Once more I heard the voice: "You came back too fast."

Not until 1948 did I take the longed-for trip to visit my family. My "Christmas journey" 23 years before had been almost forgotten until my mother took me aside one day and said, "I saw you at Christmastime in 1925. You came across the yard and looked in the window. Although it was awfully cold you were wearing only a thin dress. Why didn't you come in?"

—Agnes O. Erickson, Altamont, Illinois
October 1973

Out of Body

It was late morning on August 22, 1969, near Hiep Duc, South Vietnam. I was copilot of a four-man Dustoff, a medical evacuation helicopter crew making a tactical approach to pick up a seriously wounded American infantryman in a secluded land zone (LZ), surrounded by a well-entrenched enemy force. We began taking heavy ground fire and hits even before we landed in this tiny clearing barely wider than our rotor blades.

The chatter of enemy machine guns could be heard all around as our medic, SP5 John Seebeth, helped load our patient. At that instant he was grabbed by the throat and spun back onto the deck. He knew something was wrong, but he didn't know what. So he tried to talk over the intercom—but nothing came out. He put his hand to his throat and felt a warm, sticky substance. When he looked down, he saw that his hand was covered with blood. Automatic weapons fire had torn out his larynx and a large part of his throat.

Somehow we got out of the LZ with our patient, although additional fire ultimately shot out three of our four radios and caused other damage to the aircraft. At LZ Baldy, 25 miles south of Da Nang, I held John's legs as a doctor used a scalpel to perform a tracheotomy—without anesthetic.

John and I were reunited in 1982 in Seattle, Washington, after I'd finally located him through the Veterans Administration system 13 years later. I flew there from Lincoln, Nebraska.

John had undergone extensive surgery for the reconstruction of his larynx and was able to speak, albeit hoarsely. We had three days to relive our Vietnam experiences. For over four hours I asked questions in a taped interview about what he remembered of those three traumatic days, and especially the final mission where he received his hundred-percent disability.

"John, do you remember what happened after you were wounded?" I asked.

"Yes," he replied. "You turned around and said 'We'll get you back, John. You'll be all right.' Then I had an out-of-body experience. I was above the LZ, above the rotor blades, looking down at myself and the others in the helicopter. There was no pain. I knew I was going to die if I didn't fight to get back to my body. I looked out over the beautiful Vietnamese countryside. It wasn't threatening or negative. It was peaceful and very warm."

John had not spoken to any of our crew since he was wounded, except me, yet he went on to relate, nearly word for word, exactly what had been said over the intercom from the moment he was hit until we landed at LZ Baldy, about 10 or 12 minutes later.

Some may believe this isn't extraordinary, but it is,

because the moment John was hit he removed his flight helmet. There was no way he could have heard what any of us said over the intercom, yet he did and was able to repeat it nearly verbatim to me more than 13 years later.

—Lt. Col. Robert B. Robeson (AUS, Ret.),
Lincoln, Nebraska
January 1993

My Boy and His Spirit

Recently I became deeply dissatisfied with my job and began actively seeking a promotion. Furthermore the gloomy, overcast skies and cold weather in Illinois were depressing my wife. You can bet we were pretty darned anxious to move to a warmer, sunnier climate.

Miraculously, within one week three offers were presented to me. They were all good jobs, promotions within my company and in my field, and all in the south—where I had focused my efforts.

Each would have been a viable option for different reasons. One was in the perfect city, another was the closest to our family, and the last was offering the most money. A tough decision! My mom, a practitioner of various home remedies, suggested that before I went to sleep, I should write the title of each position on a slip of paper. Then, she advised, I should fold each slip of paper and put it under its own glass of water after first drinking half. She told me that as soon as I woke up the next morning, without looking, I should reach over and randomly grab a glass, immediately drinking it down. If the rest of the water in the glass went down easily I would know that the job that went with it was the right one.

Strange as this sounds, things got even stranger late that night. My boy Griffin is a normal four-year-old. Rambunctious, creative, cartoon-loving, and a joy to have—and after that fateful night I would add "gifted" to his list of qualities. I was awakened from a deep sleep by the sound of Griffin gently calling my name, as if from a distance. I rolled over and started to get out of bed when I saw, right before my eyes, a vision of my son glowing slightly and hovering over the three glasses, grinning his impish grin. I was astonished, to say the least. I rubbed my eyes, thinking I was dreaming, when Griffin slowly pointed down at the middle glass. Without thinking I reached down, picked up the middle glass, and downed the water easily. My boy and his grin faded away like the Cheshire Cat. I immediately felt a wave of sleepiness wash over me and fell fast asleep.

The next morning I was startled to see that the middle glass was already empty. It hadn't been a dream! Of course, I accepted that job, which was the one closest to our families, as Griffin's spirit advised. We have never been happier. We are now warm, surrounded by sun, and can visit our extended families whenever we want. It was the best decision we ever made. And Griffin, who doesn't even remember his psychic hint, deserves all the credit!

—Rev. Paul Thomas, Dallas, Texas
August 1998

I Died

I have learned two things beyond the shadow of a doubt: that there is life beyond, and that time does not exist there.

I had believed in life after death most of the time. But there is a vast gulf between believing and knowing and occasionally I caught myself wondering and dreading that plunge into the unknown which must come to all of us.

A few days before Christmas, 1948, I "died" from a violent heart seizure. My husband was with me at the time and is willing to take an oath to the truth of this statement. He has witnessed death many times and recognized the symptoms, eyes wide and staring, rattle in the throat and protruding tongue, no heartbeat, no breath.

My "dying" was painful, but of short duration and after a brief sensation of whirling about in a spiral, I found myself alone in a great vastness. I had no body, neither dense nor etheric, yet every sense was alert. I was only a consciousness, with a delicious awareness of absolute freedom, an ecstasy of lightness.

All about me was space. Yet this space was not a void but filled with the essence of all life. Since my experience I have tried to describe this; how I knew it, what it looked like. But since there is nothing on earth with which to compare it, this is most difficult and any terms I can use are unsatisfactory. I can say only that the entire space was alive. Life was there, all about me.

I was part of it, yet I was still myself, a separate and distinct entity. I could feel this marvelous essence penetrating me; could see it as a form of light, but light that was alive.

This space had color, too. But again an accurate description is impossible. The delicate glow of a sunset on a snowy peak in the high mountains, just as it passes from rose to orchid, is closest to it, I think. I floated and floated, filled with a sense of well-being.

There was also sound, of which I seemed gradually to become aware. It was a tinkle, a cadence, a delightful blending of delicate, bell-like notes. I was curious to know what caused this lovely, joyous sound. I asked and was told, by mental impression, that I was hearing the laughter of children.

Then I began to feel a gradual withdrawal. The sound was receding; the beautiful, life-filled space fading. I begged to stay. But a voice spoke with deep, melodious resonance saying, "You must go back.

You must go back. You...must...go...back." It too faded, and was gone. I was back.

"I've been gone a long time, haven't I?" I whispered to my husband.

"Only about 10 seconds," he replied, "but I thought it was forever. It's a miracle."

Ten seconds. I could scarcely believe him.

Now I no longer only believe in a life beyond the physical. I KNOW.

—Beth Dene Aldrich, Bishop, California
September 1950

Rescue by Teleportation

In August 1943 while vacationing in California, I suddenly became aware that my nephew Ellsworth Carrol and a buddy of his were in grave danger. Ellsworth was serving in an army unit involved in the invasion of Sicily. In an instant I was teleported to a spot close to a foxhole in which Ellsworth and his buddy Ralph were huddling to dodge shrapnel. At once I entered the foxhole, grabbed the two young men and hauled them out. Ellsworth was about to remonstrate against my dragging them from safety when the whine of a shell drew our attention back to the foxhole. The shell made a direct hit on their former shelter and both would have died instantly had they remained there. Then, as suddenly as I had teleported to Italy, I found myself back in California.

In November 1945 Ellsworth returned from service and the following month I traveled to his home in Cabbool, Missouri. After we had exchanged greetings Ellsworth's first question to me was: "Uncle, what battalion did you serve in during the invasion of Italy?" I replied that I had not served in Italy at all. "But, Uncle, you were there," he insisted. "You pulled me and my buddy from a foxhole while we were in Sicily. If you hadn't we both would have been killed. I turned around to thank you but you already had gone."

To this day I have been unable to convince Ellsworth that I never served with the army in Italy.

—Dewey Schley Carroll, Tennessee Ridge, Tennessee
May 1973

My Visit to Heaven's Shores

The day I died taught me how to live. I had no immediate awareness that I was dead, even though I had gone to bed feeling very ill.

I suffer from a connective tissue disease, which weakens my immune system. What would be a simple cold to most people can make me very ill. Pneumonia has left me fighting for my life more than once. Sometimes I feel I'll never escape the dark abyss.

One night, I became aware of looking down on a sleeping woman. She looked cold and pale.

"Poor thing. She looks ill," I thought. I tried to cover her but could not make my hand touch the blanket. I felt overwhelming confusion.

The woman was lying on her stomach, concealing her face, but I felt a sense of recognition. I looked at her from head to toe, but couldn't place her. Suddenly, in horror, I realized that her dark, shoulder-length hair was the hair I washed and curled every morning. It was me!

My mind raced. "If this is me, why am I up here?" I thought. I realized I was dead. I felt myself ascending rapidly. I could not see where I was going, but the weightless feeling fascinated me. I felt like an astronaut in eternity.

Two beings met me during my ascent. They were white and bright like the moonlight. They stood on either side of me and took me by the arms. We entered a tunnel. I began to wonder whether I was going to heaven or hell.

While I believed in God, I had some concerns about where I would spend eternity. I started to think legalistically, counting the times I had skipped church or forgotten to pray.

The tunnel seemed to close around us. A combination of dark and light, it was nighttime with shooting stars. I felt out of control of my own destiny, but fascinated by the beauty of the lights.

Suddenly, my guides stopped. They stood in front of me, their heads bowed as a larger light being approached. He was wearing a garment of light, and He seemed to be in control. I called Him Jesus. He neither confirmed nor denied that this was His name.

I tried to speak to this being and saw my thoughts ricochet off the top of the tunnel. They bounced over the tops of the guides and reached the head of the brighter being. Communication was with thoughts, not words. The thoughts looked like energy beams.

The Master Being spoke to me in the same way. I could hear his voice in my mind while I watched the beams of light.

"Pat," He said, "I have not yet willed you here. You have come here because of your own lack of will to live."

I considered that. I had recently experienced the death of a child, and I was still learning to cope with my own disease. My life contained little true happiness at that time.

"You are allowed to stay here if you choose," He continued. I was elated. "But I must tell you something. If you choose to enter now, there may be others who will not come, since you are not on Earth to guide them."

I wanted to stay, but I felt that I had to go back if others truly needed me. I never stated my choice, but suddenly I zoomed back through the tunnel, faster than light, and returned to my body. I sat straight up in bed, yelling, "Wow!"

In the days that followed I told my story. My doctor told me that ill people with high fevers often hallucinate. My pastor simply smiled and nodded. My friends and family were skeptical. I stopped telling the story until now.

The experience has changed the way I view life. I am less concerned with legalistic thinking and more concerned about acting from the heart. There is no reward for acting any other way; if you're looking for gain in heaven or in other people's eyes, forget it.

I have been very ill on other occasions. Two years ago, I was in a wheelchair and could not even lift my legs without help. I recovered. My doctor was amazed. Recently, I had a severe flu that led to complications. As I drifted into unconsciousness, I could see the tunnel. A flurry of angels' wings blocked the entrance—a new revelation, since the light beings in the tunnel I had entered before did not have wings. I knew that once again, it was not my time to go.

I am a kinder and gentler Pat. I visit the sick and reassure them what waits for them at the end of their journey. Once, while in the hospital, I even left my body to lead another soul to the tunnel. The young woman did not have the fear that I had experienced. She readily allowed me to show her the way to eternity. She knew it was her time to go.

I know my story sounds ridiculous to the doubter. As a therapist, I would have thought someone was psychotic for believing in out-of-body experiences and angels prior to my own experience.

You may never have an experience like mine until the moment of death. My only advice is to live life to the fullest. Act only when you feel it in your heart. Death has no victory over me now. When my life is over it will be because my work is complete. There is no fear—only hope, light, and love.

—Patricia Bowskill, Cincinnatti, Ohio
July 1998

Old Souls

Reincarnation, the belief that we possess eternal souls and live many lifetimes, is a central tenet of Hinduism and Buddhism. Most of us do not remember our past lives, and there may be a very good reason for this. If we have certain goals to achieve and lessons to learn in this lifetime, it may be that ignorance of our past lives helps us focus on the present life. But occasionally, past-life memories break through and we are allowed a glimpse of what lies beyond the veil.

My Boyfriend's Soulmate

In May of 1993 I met Mike in Ft. Myers, Florida. Something about his character and spontaneous lifestyle hooked me in just two weeks. I began to have romantic feelings for him, and dated him regularly.

My strong feelings for Mike persuaded me to express my love with the most precious words I knew, hoping he would understand my serious intentions. He felt just as I did.

Later that evening I was preparing to go out. Mike was dressed up and ready to go, leaning against the frame of my bedroom door and talking with me as I looked for shoes in the closet. Babbling on about the evening's plans, I turned to look at him and was startled. I noticed something over his shoulder, out in my living room—a woman dressed in a flowing white gown, the type worn in the 1930s.

She was standing behind him, listening to me, and watching him, studying the relationship to see if it met her standards. She startled me, but only because I saw her—then she disappeared.

I told Mike what I had seen and felt, and assured him I was not worried or frightened. Mike smiled and said, "I thought she had gone."

She had been in his life a long time. He first found out about her several years ago from a tarot reading, and then from a psychic a year later. They described her as his soulmate, a woman he had been with in a past life but never had the chance to marry, due to her untimely death during their engagement.

Mike has never seen this apparition himself. She has been seen by only one other person—Cheryl, a woman he had been in love with five years ago. She had not felt worried, and reported what the woman had worn.

Mike enjoys knowing that his soulmate's ghost is around. He believes that she protects him from untrue love. When she feels a woman is right for him, she personally checks out his prospective partner.

—Sheryl A. Kurlinski, Ft. Myers, Florida
February 1994

My Prehistoric Life

Shortly after my sixth birthday in August 1904, I told my father of a dream in which I had seen myself as a monkey-like creature playing in a dark wood. I had found and picked a bunch of cup-like, vivid blue flowers, unlike any I had ever seen. This incident alone was vastly exciting to a six-year-old, who had seen flowers only in florists' windows, vases, and parks and never had picked any.

Father taught science at the local school and was far more interested in my dream than I expected him to be. He asked if I had been looking in any of his books. When I said I had not, he showed me some pictures in *The Evolution of Man.* Later he bought a partly hatched egg from a farmer's wife—who I am sure thought we were mad and in a class with "body snatchers"—and we broke the egg into a saucer to compare the embryo inside with a plate in one of his books.

I can recall my primeval home as clearly as any in which I have lived in this life. Whether it is because of the importance Father attached to my dream or because I actually was remembering a previous existence, I do not know. I have revisited my forest home in dreams several times, always being about my actual age but quite primitive.

I clearly remember the trail to the water hole, but I do not recall ever carrying water in any kind of container, or seeing any tools except my mate's club and the shiny pronged stick on which I roasted the lumps of meat that my mate had smashed up with his club.

My dreams of this prehistoric life are, for the most part, placid, restful, and almost without incident. One dream, however, held a bit of excitement.

In this dream I was picking berries in the forest and suddenly found myself confronted by a strange male, who apparently had swung down from a tree. He seized my wrist and sought to carry me off with him. I screamed, partly in fear and partly in anger, and my mate came running from where he had been napping nearby.

When he saw the intruder, he growled in rage and

rushed at him, brandishing his club. A brief but violent battle followed. Flailing savagely with his club, my mate killed his rival. I took this calmly, as a matter of course.

Although I can wander in memory around my prehistoric home, I cannot voluntarily visit it in dreams. I often wish I could.

—Kathleen Casler, Smithers, British Columbia, Canada
April 1957

And Baby Makes Two

Being Buddhist, I've always believed in reincarnation. But when my grandfather died 16 years ago, reincarnation was the furthest thing from my mind. I chanted for him twice a day after that but never expected the spiritual bond I was creating with him by doing this to manifest itself in such a physical way.

I began hearing loud whispers inside my head. If I was falling asleep while driving, the whisper would say, "Wake up!" and I would awake. If I was still in bed when I should be up, it would say, "Cathy!" and I'd open my eyes, or if something was threatening me, the voice would say, "Look out!"

At first it seemed strange, but after a while I attributed it to an unusual function of the protective forces of the universe and welcomed it as a new facet of my life.

Ten years later my husband Benjamin and I had a beautiful baby girl, Jessica. We lived in a second floor apartment in Medway, Massachusetts. As soon as Jessica learned to walk down the stairs, I'd walk in front of her, she wouldn't fall. I thought it was so cute that at the age of two she was so protective of me, always saying, "Watch out, Mama," or "Be careful, Mama, don't fall."

It wasn't until one day two years later that it suddenly hit me: The voice inside my head was gone. When I thought back to the last time I'd heard it, I got chills all over my body. The last time I heard that voice was just before I became pregnant with my daughter.

—Cathy Mann, Tucson, Arizona
February 1993

The Egyptian Caps

One night in January 1925 while I was living in New York, I had a vivid dream in which I was standing on a partly completed Egyptian pyramid, waiting for my guide. The heat was intense. My guide I knew was a copper-skinned man wearing a blue net cap. Apparently I was a stranger, for my skin was light-colored and I wore white clothing and a white net cap similar to my guide's.

Just below me a small squat man dressed in the

remnants of a uniform was smoothing a block of stone. I found the smell of his sweat and the stone dust offensive. Farther down, a dozen men were hoisting a block up the face of the pyramid. The middle of the block teetered against the edge of one in place. They slipped a netted rope sling over the projecting lower part and hauled. The block leveled and rose easily as if on a hinge.

On the ground far below was a long wooden shelter for feeding the workers. The ground around it was watered to keep down the dust as people went to and fro. Just as my guide with the blue cap arrived, the dream ended. It made no sense to me.

I never had read anything on Egyptian history nor had I seen a museum exhibit on the subject. But shortly after my dream I visited the Metropolitan Museum of Art and in a case of exhibits from the Pyramid Period Dynasty two caps were on display, a blue one identical to that in my dream and a yellowed one that once had been white. In my edition of the *Encyclopaedia Britannica* I found a picture of a beaten-copper portrait of Prince Mer-en-ra wearing a similar cap. Archaeologists date it variously from 4700 B.C. to 3000 B.C.

In my dream did I tap the mind of an Egyptian scholar or was this perhaps a memory of a former life of mine?

—Margaret R. Law, Princeton, New Jersey
September 1973

From a Past Life

Is it possible to remember a past life? I believe I did and now I believe in reincarnation.

My friend Arthur Burch invited me to his home in November 1958, to meet a visiting relative and also a girl he identified only as "a redhead."

When I arrived I went to the door and as usual knocked twice and then went in. All I saw when I stepped into the room was the redhead—and I knew her. This picture came instantly to my mind:

She was standing halfway up a flight of marble steps leading to a columned building. She wore a white Grecian robe belted at the waist with a cord. I seemed to be wearing a white Greek tunic and standing on bare ground. From 20 feet apart we stood looking at each other. The day was sunny and dry and the picture clear and unforgettable—but in reality it was 8:00 P.M. in Mobile, Alabama.

In the home were five people: Arthur, his wife Lee, his brother Steve, his brother whom he introduced as "Burch," and Shirley Adkins, the very attractive young redhead.

Arthur came toward me saying, "Oh, you two know each other?"

Suddenly I became aware of where I was and replied, "No, I've never seen her before." She agreed. Then I asked him why he had asked. He said,

"Well, someone seeing your faces would think you had met before."

It was obvious to everyone there that we actually did recognize each other. And later, after Shirley and I were married, she confessed she had shared my vision that night, seeing everything I had seen down to the last detail.

—Carl Knodel, Mobile, Alabama
October 1970

My Mother Returns

In 1972, a car stalled on the hill in front of our house and Kathy, my ex-wife (who returned to live with me), asked if there was anything she could do—did they want to use the phone or come in? They did. They were three or four young men and women who had just come back from India, where they had seen Sathya Sai Baba.

They were just leaving the Baba Center, a few blocks away, on their way home to San Francisco.

They showed Kathy a ring Baba had manifested for one of the young women. He opened his hand and she saw a large gold ring with his picture on it. She said that it was a man's ring, so he closed his hand and opened it again, and there was a very small ring in its place. She said, "Quit teasing me," so he blew on it, and it gradually grew bigger until it was just the right size. Then they gave us a picture of Sai Baba.

We started to go to the Baba Center occasionally and got all of the books we could find on him, becoming interested in his life story.

One day a fellow from the center came by our house with some liquid *vibhuties*. Baba manifests an ash, and sometimes a sweet, tasty, honey-like liquid to bless people with. Both are called *vibhuties*.

My mother, Anna Leininger Stiess, was spending a few days with us. He put a teaspoonful on our tongues, but my mother's portion spilled all over her new white knit dress, upsetting her.

Two weeks later, in 1973, when I went to work in the emergency room, one of the paramedics said that he was sorry to learn that my mother had been killed.

Confused, I asked him how he knew that, and he showed me an article on the second page of the Los Angeles Times, describing how a dump truck had skidded across the double line, hitting her car head-on and killing her instantly!

She was a widow living alone in Garden Grove, 50 miles from Los Angeles. Why did they write an article about her? I was not notified because the Orange County police did not know who her next of kin was. We went to the mortuary to claim her body and arrange the funeral.

When we came home that night and turned down the covers on the bed, the whole room suddenly filled with a strong odor of Baba's vibhuties.

I felt this meant that he made sure she had a peaceful passing.

Mother had been very involved in the care of her adopted granddaughter, Diane Von Habsburg. My sister, Anna Chapman, could not have children, so I had arranged for Anna to adopt a baby girl (Diane) delivered from a mother who did not want the child. My mother and sister raised her, and when Diane was 20 years old, she was in a severe auto accident and became a paraplegic.

Mother, my sister Anna, and my sister's chauffeur took care of Diane, and she eventually married the chauffeur.

In 1975, two years after my mother was killed, Diane delivered a healthy child, Alexandria Von Habsburg. In 1978, when she was two or three years old, Alexandria started noticing things that had belonged to my mother. She would say, "Oh, that used to be my ring," or "I used to have a piano like that one."

One day they were out driving and she said, "If you turn here, I'll show you where I used to live. Turn here—that's my house," and she pointed to my mother's old house. Pictures taken of her at the age of eight are identical to pictures of my mother at that age, even to how she combed her hair. I feel my mother came back to continue to care for her grandchild, Diane.

—Walter Steiss, M.D., Van Nuys, California
August 1993

Memories of Egypt

I was eight years old when I first began to tell strange tales to the other children. Every night we got together in a large group to tell stories. When it was my turn I told the usual ghost stories but the day came when I started to tell ghost stories of old Egypt.

The other kids stopped telling stories and came to my house every night to hear my stories instead. Even the grown people listened.

I had never heard of Egypt or its tombs before. But in my stories I told of the curse of the tombs. I told of the Sphinx and the Pyramid. I described the inside with its chambers and long silent halls. I told of the Pharaohs who were buried within and I also described a mummy. I told of the Nile River and described it in detail. I told of the temple of Karnak. I told of the key stone and the seal on the tombs.

I told of an enemy that attacked the Egyptians and was driven off time and time again. Then as a last hope the enemy killed many cats and tied them to their shields knowing that the cat was sacred to the Egyptian people. When this army again marched against Egypt, the Egyptians, seeing the cats, fled in horror.

When I went to high school I found in my history book a cutaway section of the pyramid that showed it to be just like I had said. Reading on I found that everything else had been just as I had described it.

But my biggest shock was yet to come. Later in the term our teacher told the story of the Egyptian army fleeing before an enemy who had cats tied to their shields.

Does this prove that we come back to live on Earth again? I think it does.

—Hugh O. Griffin, Portsmouth, Virginia
September 1950

A Death Revisited

In 1970 I was a member of a small study group that met weekly in Cleveland, Ohio, for psychic research. One of our members, Robert Howitt, was a highly successful hypnotist but refused to use his ability indiscriminately or merely for entertainment. We had talked often of conducting an experiment in past-life regression and one February evening finally undertook one.

Eight of us were gathered in the home of Betty Metzel, one of our members. Howitt had brought a Brain Wave Synchronizer to help induce trance. After he had explained briefly how it worked the experiment got underway. We tried first one subject and then another but none could get beyond a fully relaxed state.

I had no difficulties, however. I could feel my consciousness ebbing as soon as I faced the machine.

While the hypnotist's voice droned on, a tape recorder was started to record the session. After some initial suggestions to relax and to remember everything upon awakening I was guided carefully back in time. I remembered my seventh-grade teacher, my first day of school, and listening to a radio when I was an infant. Then I was instructed to go further back in time. Gray-black clouds seemed to swirl about me.

Suddenly there was darkness and I was in a thick woods with large trees looming around me. I was a terribly frightened young soldier holding a rifle and sitting in a hole in the ground with my knees tight against my chest. As questions were put to me at this point I registered disgust and impatience. Obviously I was a Confederate soldier and I seemed concerned the Yankees might overhear my answers. I knew it was September of 1862 but I was not sure where I was. I knew only that our army under General Lee recently had crossed the Potomac River from Virginia into Maryland.

I was reassured that I was perfectly safe and the questions continued. I was from near Lexington, Kentucky, and had enlisted the previous summer. I was 19 years old. When asked if I were in pain, I replied, "My legs...damned cramped in this hole." My replies were in a low drawling voice with gasps and long pauses. I was perspiring heavily. As the questioning continued, my voice began to crack with fear and discomfort. My replies became even more abrupt, my heavy breathing became panting. I was in mortal terror for my life.

The hypnotist (who had his dates confused) asked me about Lincoln's assassination. I hadn't heard of it, I gasped, but hoped it was true. I also was asked about my weapon, which ironically was a Union rifle I had picked up somewhere. Further questioning was useless; vague forms were moving in the trees and I was paralyzed with fright. Suddenly enemy cavalry burst from behind the trees. I wanted to scream in a wild frenzy.

The hypnotist rightly concluded we had gone far enough and quickly led me back through swirling clouds to the present. With the final suggestion that I was all right and would remember all that had occurred he awakened me. My legs felt terribly sore; I was covered with perspiration and still very scared. It seemed as if I had been snatched from a battlefield at a terrifying moment.

I often have thought of my experience that night and I believe I received personal proof of reincarnation. I know that a young man died a horrible death in September 1862 and that young man and I are the same person.

—Daniel A. Schreiner, Brooklyn, Ohio
December 1972

Pain of a Former Life

When I left home in March 1973 for a four-week vacation in India I hoped to learn something about reincarnation. I didn't disbelieve—nor could I fully accept it.

After a week in Bombay I spent three days in Aurangabad exploring the Ellora and Ajunta Caves. (These are not really caves but beautifully carved and painted temples.) In the most impressive one, the Kailasa Temple, a sudden burst of pain between my eyebrows brought tears to my eyes. As the pain grew more intense I wept like an old woman on the verge of a nervous breakdown.

My guide, Ishtiaq Quraishi, looked at me in bewilderment, then gently seated me on a bench. With a glance of understanding he silently disappeared into the shadows.

My thoughts turned to reincarnation. In some past life had I worked on this massive rock sculpture and possibly fallen to my death? When Ishtiaq reappeared he insisted on photographing me where I sat. When I asked, "Why?" he replied, "So you will never forget!" As if I could!

I toured southern India for two weeks, then decided to return to the Kailasa Temple to attempt to solve the riddle. I wanted to question Ishtiaq further but because I had not wired ahead I did not see him. I was disappointed but the manager secured another guide for me and all went smoothly until we approached the Kailasa Gates. As I kicked off my shoes to enter I started to tremble, feeling smothered in a cloak of depression. I didn't know what I was getting into but felt I must explore the mystery of these feelings.

We walked into the main temple which is supported by a sculptured frieze of elephants. I ran my hands over them, thinking I would feel a rapport or some sense of recall. I got nothing!

Eventually we reached the second level and again I started to cry. My guide turned to me compassionately and said softly, "Oh, you are the weeping lady. Ishtiaq told me about you. I am so sorry." Then he faded into the shadows. The pain between my eyebrows struck again, soon reached its peak, then subsided. I thought, "What a dumb thing to do! I'll never get an answer here." I called the guide and we left the temple.

I had been home in Illinois only a few days when my friend Phyl Anderson called from Wisconsin to say that she had discovered a "wonderful psychic" in Madison. She had made an appointment for me to see her the following day.

When I walked into the room for my consultation, the psychic Stephanie said, "My, what a wonderful experience you have had!"

Thinking Phyl had told her about my travels I replied, "Yes, it was quite a trip."

"No, no," she said, "I did not mean that. You went

to India to find out about reincarnation. Don't you know you were killed in that very same temple? You were a dealer in precious and semiprecious stones. Your best friend bashed in your head at that very spot and took all your gems!"

I drove home deep in thought and went straight to my bedroom where I pulled out three large boxes and stared at their contents. All kinds of jewelry! I always had had a deep love for precious and semiprecious stones and had collected them all my life. I rarely wear them but revel in their glitter and smooth, cool surfaces. Is this from a former life?

I went to bed that night exhausted and slept soundly. In the morning I was astonished to see in the mirror an enormous red bump between my eyebrows! There was no way I could hide or explain it. I am a firm believer in reincarnation.

—Karen Hudson, Bellwood, Illinois
October 1975

The Time Curtain

I would like to tell you about something that happened to me 12 years ago. It is my belief that during this experience I had a short journey into another time period.

It was warm, the sun was shining—there was a slight breeze blowing—a typical July country day.

By mid-afternoon I was finishing up my daily chores and had left the house carrying a bag of wastepaper in each hand. I was heading for the burning area to dispose of them, not thinking about anything in particular other than what I was going to prepare for dinner.

As I left the patio and started walking, I became aware of hearing a sound that I hadn't heard for some time, the unmistakable sound of horses. That was not unusual since I live in the middle of a 60-acre farm, and throughout the years that I have been here, a few of the neighboring farms have kept horses. It used to be that the sound of a couple of riders on horseback crossing our property was not unusual. I would occasionally hear a horse whinnying in the distance from either of these farms.

I hadn't heard this sound for some time, but there was no mistaking the distinct sound of running horses.

I kept on walking, and as I did, the sound of thundering hooves grew louder, coming in my direction. It quickly became clear that these horses weren't just running fast, they were moving at great speed. In no time at all, the sound got much louder and closer. I didn't take time to look around to see how close they were, but suddenly I knew that those horses were approaching swiftly, and that great danger was very near.

I had no time to think and could only react.

Knowing that I had to get out of the way fast, I made a tremendous leap to the side, scattering the contents of the bags I was carrying and sprawling on the ground.

In the roar and confusion of the moment, when the horses passed the spot where I had been only seconds before, I saw a chariot with a driver and four horses in a cloud of dust, careening away into the distance.

I picked myself up and gathered up the contents of the bags in slow motion. I was stunned and dumbfounded, and walked back into the house in a daze.

My teenage daughter, Kaye, and her boyfriend, James Ulp of Milton, Massachusetts, were in the house. They took one look at my face, which was as white as a sheet, and asked excitedly, "What happened to you?"

I told them what had happened the best that I could, but was at a loss to explain what it meant at that time.

I now know that I unwittingly stumbled into the opening of a time curtain and that I was drawn into it, reliving an experience from a past life.

Since that time I have learned that curtains between this world and the past do exist. They are only visible for a short time. At other times they are sensed, but not seen with the physical eye.

—Sara M. Phleger, Milton, Massachusetts
April 1993

My Other Lives

I have had numerous experiences that lead me to believe that I have lived before—many times. In my first past-life experience I saw scenes that led me to believe that I was an officer in the Japanese navy during World War II.

It began in 1968. After serving a year with the air force in Vietnam, I was assigned to Yakota Air Base outside Tokyo, Japan. During my year in Vietnam I also had spent time in Thailand and the Philippines. In these three countries I heard the inhabitants speak in their native tongues that to me always sounded like nonsensical gibberish.

An interesting thing happened, however, after I arrived in Japan. I was sitting in a bar one night and at the next table two other servicemen sat with two Japanese women. The women could speak English but not fluently. When they spoke to each other in Japanese I found the sounds they were making formed definite words and were not a mishmash of unintelligible noise. I even understood what they were saying; they were discussing how they were going to hustle these two servicemen. This impression was validated later that evening when I saw the same two servicemen, alone this time, grumbling about having been taken for some money. After this experience I began to listen carefully whenever the natives spoke.

I bought several books and began learning to speak Japanese. I learned easily and began to think I was some kind of whiz kid who could learn a language overnight. (I subsequently disproved this theory when I almost failed Spanish in college.)

Within a couple of months I could converse in Japanese and thereafter taught myself to read and write Japanese. I even found myself dreaming in Japanese.

After a little more than a year I had the experience that tuned me into a life I lived during World War II. The North Koreans shot down a U.S. Navy surveillance plane over disputed international waters. The air force sent my squadron of jet fighters to Korea to beef up the U.S. forces there. I was a mechanic and traveled to South Korea in a C-130 propeller-driven cargo plane along with the equipment we would need to maintain the planes.

Over the Sea of Japan a pressurization panel blew off the plane and the craft suddenly dived toward the water below. The sudden depressurization caused a tremendous pain in my head; I thought my eardrums would pop. Agony mixed with fear was written on everyone's face. Many began to faint. The crew chief came running to the back of the plane to determine the damage. He fainted at my feet. The whine of the plane as it descended was deafening.

At this point I relived my death during World War II. The man at my feet was now a Japanese. We were flying in a Mitsubishi bomber that had just been strafed by an American P-38. The gunner was hit, fell out of the gun turret, and landed at my feet.

I scrambled up the ladder to the gun turret. I was no longer 20 years old; I was in my fifties and slightly overweight. I was wearing the white uniform of a Japanese naval officer. I seemed quite familiar with the gun as I took sight on an approaching P-38. I aimed for the cockpit; the bullets found their mark and the P-38 went out of control. There were three other Mitsubishis and what seemed like dozens of P-38s in the air around us. I took aim at several of the P-38s and saw some of them dive toward the ocean with black smoke billowing behind them.

Now several P-38s flew toward my plane and opened up; the bullets ripped through the metal around me. I was thrown back against the wall and fell out of the turret, landing on the body of the gunner. I tried to climb back up the ladder but my body wouldn't respond. All I could hear was a deafening whine as the plane fell.

Suddenly the present-day whine stopped. The pilot leveled off the C-130 at a low altitude where we could fly without pressurization.

But after this experience with a past life I was disoriented. I didn't know who I was. I would forget where I was going and what I was doing. Scenes from my life in World War II kept flashing into my mind. The overriding feeling I got from the whole experience was a tremendous sense of guilt for ordering people to death.

I finally went to a psychiatrist who, not knowing anything about past lives, determined that I was having an "area reaction." I was sent back to the States and it is true I never had any further problems.

These experiences served as a stimulus and I began a search to understand them. I read a series of books by Ernest L. and Ruth E. Norman; the most helpful was *The Infinite Concept of Cosmic Creation*. I began to see the validity of reincarnation. It is all quite logical. Science has proven that energy cannot be destroyed; it can only be changed. If energy animates our physical bodies, then this energy too is subject to the laws of nature and cannot be destroyed, only changed. Perhaps the manner in which we live our lives determines whether we refine this energy source or pervert it. When man begins to understand the consequences of his acts the world will become a saner place in which to live.

—Dennis C. Dallison, El Cajun, California
April 1984

Ghosts, Hauntings, and other Tales of the Spirit World

Have you ever seen a ghost? Perhaps you've experienced strange phenomena like unexplained cold spots or disappearing objects. Or perhaps you don't believe that ghosts exist at all. So did many of the authors in this chapter. Until one day, something changed their minds. . .

Phantom Carriage

Back in 1917 when I was seven years old and my brother nine, we were living in an isolated section of the north of Ireland. As is customary there we helped with the farm work after coming home from school. This particular July evening our task was to go to the bog and place the recently cut peat in small lumps so as to hasten drying. As the evening wore on and all the other workers had gone home, daylight giving way to the long twilight of that northern latitude, my brother looked up and exclaimed, "Look, Johnnie, what's that?" I turned in the direction he pointed and there not more than fifty yards from where we were working on marshy and impassable terrain appeared an animal-drawn vehicle. I say animal-drawn because it seemed too small for either horse or donkey. The vehicle itself was somewhat like a trap. Its lone occupant sat facing us and seemed to have neither interest nor control over the destination or behavior of the animal drawing it.

Our amazement grew as it seemed to change in appearance as it moved away from us. Now there were two occupants. The vehicle itself took on a coach-like shape. Across the uneven, marshy waste-land definitely impassable for any normal vehicle this strange spectacle passed, oblivious of the numerous turfbanks that crossed its path until it faded out of sight in the distance. We were transfixed for a few moments. Then fear overtook us and we ran wildly home to relate our experience to our parents, who laughed at our story.

Some years later when we were able to get our teacher to listen to this strange tale, he attempted to explain it as a form of mirage. He said that the vehicle we saw was really a normal one passing along a road beyond the horizon which was parallel to the course we saw it, and that the numerous changes we saw it undergo were illusions caused by the reflected light.

This was the best explanation we ever got; however, in the thirty years that have elapsed since, my brother and I often discuss this phenomenon that we witnessed in our childhood.

—John Bonner, Brooklyn, New York
May 1950

Haunted High School

In July of 1986 I started working for a local security company in Newark, Ohio. I was promoted to sergeant and assigned to work the night shift at the high school, which sits on several acres of land, and has eight buildings with connecting underground tunnels.

The first few months went well, but then I noticed strange things happening. Every morning between 2 and 3 A.M., someone would start knocking, pulling hard on the door of the building I was in. I ran to see who it was, only to find no one anywhere. Then it began happening right in front of me without anyone on the other side of the door.

I didn't tell a soul until things grew worse. I heard footsteps in hallways behind me and people talking in locked rooms. The temperature would get very cold in certain areas of the buildings.

Finally I had a chance to train a new guard to work on my nights off. On the night I was showing him the area, we were walking through the industrial arts building hall when he noticed a man in one of the rooms. I thought it might be the janitor staying late to clean, so I attempted to open the door—it was locked. I opened it and we entered. We both saw the image of a man wearing a brown, checked, flannel shirt disappear before us. The new man quit immediately.

Other guards noticed lights going on and off in locked buildings. Locked doors were opened, rooms were cold, and an uneasy feeling pervaded some buildings. We found footprints in the snow, starting out from locked buildings and disappearing in the middle of a sidewalk, or beginning in the middle of sidewalks and going to locked rooms.

One unfortunate janitor stayed late to clean up after a basketball game. At 3 A.M. he called to ask if I had let a female student into the gym. A young girl had walked past silently, without noticing him. He couldn't find her anywhere and the only way she might have entered was if someone had let her in. We searched the gym for an hour, but found no one.

Other guards and I would hear the sound of desks being moved in rooms, and upon investigating, find nothing. We also heard people running in the halls, our names being called, and would get a bad feeling about being followed or watched.

Checking into the possible reasons for this activity, I found that in the 1960s, when the school was being built, a contractor had hanged himself in one of the buildings. In the early 1970s, a boy had been struck and killed by lightning at 2:30 P.M., directly in front of the doors that were being pulled on. The door knocking always started between 2 and 3 A.M.

We lost five guards and no one would work the school. I left that job in February of 1990 and never go near the campus, day or night.

—Donald L. Carico, Newark, Ohio
July 1993

Haunted By a Lion

One of the ghosts that haunted the old house in Northern Ireland in which my family lived from 1865 to 1888 was that of a lion, although this ghost was seen less often than the other ghosts. But as the outgoing tenant said to my father after he had signed a ten-year lease, the ghosts were well-bred ghosts and would not offend the most delicate-minded. He added that to counterbalance the ghosts was the fact that the house was a very lucky house financially. Both these statements proved true. We saw all the ghosts and after father's death 62 years later the house fetched twice what he had paid for it.

Our family was divided into two parts by the death of three children in the middle. My mother did not want the younger half to know about the ghosts, but we heard whispers and guessed the rest. For instance, I heard of the ghost of the lion the day a man called to see Father, who was engaged at the moment.

The maid showed this man up to the drawing room to await Father's coming. As was customary the maid brought up a silver salver bearing a decanter of twenty-five-year-old whiskey, a glass or two, and told the gentleman to help himself. When she left the room to return downstairs she failed to close the door from which a view of the next flight of stairs up could be seen easily.

Father was delayed and when he at last came in he was horrified to hear a yell of sheer terror. He, my mother, and the maid all dashed upstairs wondering what had happened. There was a round table in the middle of the room covered by a tablecloth that reached the floor, as was the custom in Victorian times. The man was not in view when they reached the drawing room, but the cloth stirred and the man peeped out from behind its folds. My father took the man's shaking hand and pulled him to his feet. "In God's name, what's up?" he asked.

The man stuttered, "I knew you kept hounds but I never knew that you kept lions."

Father was quick-witted and guessed at once what had happened but he did not want this man to go forth and tell his yarn. He helped the man into a chair and poured him a "nip." Then he pretended to notice how much of the whiskey had vanished. He said, "How many glasses of this whiskey did you drink?"

"Three or four, I think," the man said, in trembling accents.

"Well, my poor fellow, that accounts for it. This whiskey is 24 years old. It is not the kind served at bars. It is more than double strength. It tastes like velvet, but it is the stuff to make you see pink elephants." Father shook his head sadly.

"Oh God, is that it?" the man cried. So shaken was he that he asked my father to go with him while he signed the pledge. He had seen the lion as plain as day walk down the stairs and pause at the door to lift his lip at him, so he had dived under the tablecloth. We had many a good laugh at that.

One Sunday in 1884 as we all sat at dinner after morning church service, Mother asked my sister Athena, who was eight years my senior, to run upstairs and fetch a clean handkerchief from her room. As Athena ran upstairs and reached the next to the last landing she heard someone coming down the stairs. She wondered who it could be as all the family were at dinner and the maid was serving. Now the attic stairs were cut off by a door. Athena saw this door open and the lion step out. Athy was unable to move or cry out. The lion stretched and yawned, then turned and padded down the short flight. When it reached Athy, who was outspread against the wall, it paused and lifted its lip, showing its teeth, but it made no sound. It gave forth a heavy stench.

The lion passed her and continued down the stairs. Athy almost fell against the banister as she watched it pad downward. When it reached the foot of the stairs it pushed open the heavy oak door and went outside. Then Athy found tongue and raised the roof.

We all pounded upstairs to see what had happened. Mother did not want us younger children to hear about this and pushed Athy into a bedroom. Father ordered us all down to finish our dinner. This happened long before the incident of the man and the whiskey. When Athy and Mother returned to the table nothing further was said of the incident and we dared not ask.

After we were grown we heard the story of how, shortly after my parents were married, Father's two sisters came in 1866 to stay a month or two. One day after luncheon they went to their room to dress to go out. When Emily finished and opened the door to go down she saw the lion and screamed. Amelia joined her at the door and also saw the lion padding down the stairs. She joined in the screaming.

Father and Mother raced upstairs to see what was wrong. Emily and Amelia babbled about lions in the house. Father explained that it was only the harmless ghost of a lion they saw. But they packed up and left that evening. They did not relish the thought of living in the house with even the ghost of a lion.

As to how the lion came to haunt the house, we supposed a returning Crusader brought the lion from the Holy Land as a gift to the local chieftain. It was common knowledge that men went from our town to the Crusades and our house was old even then.

—D. J. S., Dallas, Texas
June 1954

Gratitude in a Rice Bag

In Shanghai back in 1935 when my father was a boy, my grandfather had a friend, Son Soh-Chow, whom he spent much time and money helping. The friend died eventually but sometime later my Aunt May started to fall into strange trances. Huge beads of sweat would pour from her face as she spoke in Son Soh-Chow's voice.

The family gathered around May during these trances and heard Son make numerous predictions.

All of them came true. But the family worried about May, for the trances seemed to distress her.

One day my grandfather had an overwhelming compulsion to buy a certain bag of rice. He took it home and the family began using it. The next time May went into trance Son Soh-Chow's voice spoke to my grandfather. "I tried so hard to make you buy that bag of rice. Now I have succeeded. Look in the bag and you will find a large amount of money. I am truly grateful for what you have done to help me and this is a token of my appreciation since I could not pay you back while on your plane."

Sure enough, under the next scoop of rice was a sack of money.

Although he appreciated the strange gift, my grandfather asked his friend to leave them because May was getting frail and weak from the strain of the trances. The spirit left and they heard from him no more. His debt had been paid.

—Julia L. Chu, La Jolla, California
January 1971

Ouija Board Speaks

The murder of a fourteen-year-old girl in Poway, California, in May 1967, shook the small community to its roots, but some eighth-grade girls were part of a greater mystery than the murder.

My daughter Marcia and five of her girlfriends attended a slumber party on December 29, 1966, at the home of Kathy Trantham. Marcia took along our Ouija board—often a source of fun for the girls at their parties.

They asked the usual questions about their boyfriends, but Marcia told me the next day of an especially odd message they received from the Ouija board. At one point Gail Nolan and Ellen Shumway were having their turn and they asked who was speaking through the board.

It spelled out, "The spirit of Niki Benedict." I did not know this name but my daughter explained that Niki was an eighth-grader too, new in Poway and only one or two of the girls even knew who she was.

Then Gail and Ellen asked the board, "But how can you be the spirit of Niki Benedict? She isn't dead!" The board replied, "She will be after her house burns down."

I agreed with Marcia that it was strange, but then I forgot all about it—as did the girls.

Five months later on May 1, a young boy walking home from school came upon the unconscious body of Niki Benedict. She had been stabbed twice and died on the way to the hospital without regaining consciousness. The murder is still unsolved.

The local newspaper in reporting the murder related that Niki's family had moved to Poway in the fall of 1966 after their house in Fallbrook, California, burned down.

—Betty P. Schumacher, Lompoc, California
January 1969

The Phantom Fitz

The Great Lakes ore carrier *Edmund Fitzgerald* sank in eastern Lake Superior on November 10, 1975, during a bad storm. All hands were lost. Its remains were not positively identified until May 21, 1976. But on Halloween night, October 31, 1980, my boyfriend Jerome Renner and I saw the Fitz.

The city of Duluth is built on the hills around the west end of Lake Superior and a scenic route at the top of the hills runs the length of the city. That Halloween night my boyfriend drove along Skyline Drive and stopped for a panoramic view of the city.

In the harbor we saw a stationary ore boat. It was not parallel to the docks as boats usually are but at a funny angle. All American boats show a specific individual light pattern at night and none is duplicated, especially after a sinking. We recognized the carrier as the *Edmund Fitzgerald.*

For such a large ore carrier to enter the harbor, the aerial bridge has to be raised. Jerry later talked with the men on the bridge. They told him they saw the boat coming, signaling to raise the bridge. They acknowledged and raised it. They told Jerry they could hear the sounds of sledgehammers opening the hatches as the boat passed under.

The phantom ship was gone without a trace the next day.

—Wendy Mitchell, Duluth, Minnesota
February 1988

Golden Wedding Ring

I am a treasure hunter. My favorite places to search (I use a metal detector) are around old homes. As can be imagined, I have encountered many strange haunted houses and even stranger people. One of my weirdest experiences occurred in July 1970.

I was visiting my friend James Rothrock in Hardinsburg, Kentucky, when he suggested we search an old abandoned four-room log house that was said to be haunted. Local stories told of a screaming woman who could be heard and occasionally seen around the cabin at night.

Taking a rifle and a metal detector, James, my son Michael, and I walked over to this old dwelling about noon one Sunday. We searched the yard and finding nothing of value we went inside. Pieces of antique furniture, broken glass, and the usual debris of an abandoned home were everywhere. After looking under the rugs, along the walls, and in the fireplace and finding nothing of value, we started up a flight of inside steps to the second floor.

At the top step I lifted up the old linoleum rug. About 18 inches back under it lay a woman's gold wedding ring. (I have found many unusual items during the last 30 years and the ring seemed unimportant.) I dropped it into my pocket and proceeded to search the room on the right. After finding a few items of value, I started into the room on the left of the stairway.

At the doorway I felt a rush of cold air although the temperature was in the nineties. Also I seemed to hear faint voices in the room, as if a woman and man were arguing. Mike and James told me later that they heard nothing. As I tried to enter the room, I distinctly felt a hand push against my chest, lightly but firmly, so that I could not move forward. I made three attempts to go through the doorway but was pushed back each time. Michael could actually see the indentations being made on my shirt by an unseen hand. Both Michael and my friend, however, were able to go in and out of the room easily.

After five attempts to enter the room I told Michael to get the rifle. When he handed it to me, I pumped 15 rounds into the room, breaking glass and plaster, and creating general havoc. Twice more I tried to enter the room but the unseen hand still pushed me out. James and Michael both suggested we leave.

I went home to Indiana later that day and the incident was forgotten until about two years later when a lady psychic from Ohio was visiting me. I remembered the strange circumstances surrounding my visit to the old log cabin and the ring I had found.

I handed psychic Betty Chandler the gold ring, telling her nothing of where, how, or when I had obtained it. Instantly she threw it to the floor and said, "There's blood on it and it feels as if it is on fire. The woman who wore this ring is dead; she was killed by a blow on the head from her husband and her body was hidden."

I had no idea of the identity of the woman who had owned the ring, if she was dead or even if she was married.

A few weeks later I visited Hardinsburg again. This time I talked with the owner of the old cabin site. He told me that about 30 years earlier, a man and his wife had lived in the big log house. One morning the man visited the present landowner and told him, "If you'll pay the taxes you can have my farm because I am leaving." Leave he did and was never seen again.

A short time after the man left, screams began to be heard around the house at night, and what appeared to be a woman in a long gown was seen running across the yard. A few months later, after a number of reports of the screams and the apparition had come into his office, the county sheriff investigated the site. The floor in one room of the cabin was taken up and beneath the boards they found the partially decayed skeleton of a woman dressed in the remains of a long nightgown. Identification of the body was made through a wristwatch and dental work; she was the former landowner's wife. Although the police spent years searching for him, the dead woman's husband was never found.

For some strange reason, after I found the ring about 12 years ago—I still have it—the screams ceased and nothing unusual has occurred around the old cabin. Does the ring carry a psychic message from the murdered woman? Does she want me to do something? Why couldn't I enter the room?

And last, how could the psychic possibly have known the circumstances surrounding the ring when I showed it to her?

—Michael Paul Henson, Jeffersonville, Indiana
May 1984

The Phantom Buggy

Back in 1930, during Christmas vacation, I visited my cousin Phil on the farm. I was ten at the time and Phil was nine. I always enjoyed my visits there.

One day Uncle Joe went into town to buy the few necessities he couldn't produce on the farm. Phil and I begged to go but Aunt Sue was busy with her Christmas baking so we had to stay home to do the outside chores, to feed and water the stock.

During the day a heavy rain fell which soon iced over. It made walking dangerous and difficult and we didn't finish our evening chores until after dark. We ate a late supper and put Uncle Joe's plate in the "warming closet" of the big range. We went into the living room where Phil and I sat on the floor eating nuts. Aunt Sue read Christmas stories aloud to us. After a while she stopped reading and listened. We heard the steady clop, clop of a horse's hooves on the hard frozen road. As we listened it drew nearer.

Aunt Sue laid aside her book. "That's Joe; there ain't another horse in the country that walks like ours."

Phil and I ran to the door to look out but it was so dark we couldn't see anything. Trixie, Uncle Joe's little "rat dog," squeezed out past us and ran out to greet his master.

"You boys close the door and get your coats on," called Aunt Sue. "Then light the lantern and bring in the groceries, while Joe stables the horse. I'll go warm up the coffee; I know he's cold."

I went out on the back porch to get the lantern while Phil got our coats from the closet. As I closed the door I heard the buggy turning into the yard. Before I could light the lantern there was a furious barking in the backyard. The horse snorted, and I thought someone called to the dog. Being nearer the door Aunt Sue opened it. In rushed Trixie, shaking violently and growling low in his throat.

"The horse must have stepped on his tail," laughed Aunt Sue. "See how he's shaking?"

She continued to prepare Uncle Joe's supper. "You boys run on out and unload that buggy, like I told you."

Carrying the lantern, Phil and I inched our way across the icy yard toward the buggy shelter. When we were nearly there, Phil raised the lantern high. Then he said in a shaky voice, "Jay, I don't see the buggy!"

I looked. There was no buggy. Nor could I see Uncle Joe or the horse. In spite of our fear of the dark we searched the entire yard and the stables. There was no sign of them. We couldn't find the slightest track to show us that a buggy had been there.

We went back into the house and told Aunt Sue. She thought we were joking. Her curiosity aroused, she went to take a look. She found nothing.

We all went back into the house. For the rest of the night we sat huddled near the fire, not talking above a whisper and jumping at the slightest sound.

Early the next morning a deputy sheriff came to tell us Uncle Joe was dead. The bridge across Buck Creek, weakened by the heavy winter rains, had collapsed just as he started across on his way home. Uncle Joe and the horse were drowned.

—J. T. Oliver, Columbus, Georgia
September 1950

Murder Reenacted

The Pennsylvania Dutch tell interesting ghost stories, and I have thought many times that the storytellers just might be telling the truth. This was my reaction the evening I sat in a gas station in Schaefferstown, in the heart of Lebanon County, and heard Russell Ruhl, an old-timer in the area, tell of the "Brendle murder."

It seems that back in the early 1800s a family named Brendle started to farm the land just west of town. They built two barns and a house. The barns have since been replaced but the house still stands, practically as built, the front part log, the rear stone. Shortly after the family was settled and a routine had been established the older brother took offense at something the younger one had done. One evening, calling his brother downstairs, he sank a hatchet in the back of the youngster's head. Instead of falling dead the boy ran screaming down the quarter mile lane and fell dead on the highway. The older brother disappeared and the murder went unpunished.

The story old man Ruhl told about what he had seen one night while spending a week in the old house on a bet was enough to curdle my blood. He claimed that on his third night in the house, which has stood empty 90 percent of the time since the murder, he saw the transparent forms of the brothers reenact the murder, complete with blood and screams. He claimed that he fainted and only awakened the next morning when he could find no trace of what had gone on during the night.

When he finished his story several other men sitting around the station avowed that they had known people who had seen the same apparition. In fact, it seemed that the "ghosts walked" at fairly regular intervals. At the time I wondered if perhaps the local blades made a sport of suckering someone into spending a night in the old place and then scaring the daylights out of him with a little play-acting.

Several days later I told the story to a friend of mine, Richard McDermot. He had a really good idea. He suggested turning the old house into a nightclub, using the haunted house motif, perhaps complete with a reenactment of the murder as a sort of floorshow. We became immediately enthusiastic about this enterprise and decided to visit the house the next afternoon to see how much work had to be done, and to try to find the present owner.

We agreed to meet at the farm the next afternoon but, between running into out-of-town relatives and suffering a flat tire with no spare, I arrived at the farm after dark. I did not expect to find Dick there but I took a flashlight and started to cross the field anyway. The house and barns are hidden from the road by a hill so I didn't see Dick's car behind the barn until I was within 50 feet of it. He had trusted the lane enough to drive in.

As I saw the car I also heard someone call out. Thinking Dick had seen me I was about to answer when I heard someone screaming, *"Hilfin Ich! Mein kopf, mein kopf!"* ("Help me! My head, my head!") Knowing Dick didn't speak German I immediately assumed that he had jumped a neighbor or someone for some reason known only to himself. This thought had just crossed my mind when Dick rounded the corner of the barn running at full tilt. He almost knocked me over. When he saw me in front of him he gave a chilling yell and broke off at a right angle, never slowing a bit. I took out after him and managed to stop him after about a hundred yards.

When he finally was able to speak all he would say was, "Buy the damned place and run it. Leave me out! I've had enough!"

I got him into my car and then went back for his. He wouldn't go near the place again. When we finally got settled in a local restaurant I got his story. Dick had seen exactly what the old farmer had seen 60 years before. I had not seen a thing, but those screams will stick with me the rest of my life.

About a week later I found the owner, only to be told that he had sold the place the previous day to a young Amish couple. It looks like I've tabled the nightclub plans for good, for more than one reason.

—Donald Mann, Lebanon, Pennsylvania
April 1960

Is Anybody There?

This past spring, I decided to start spring cleaning, since I had two weeks to spare before exams. I started with the inside of the house, and then worked on the yard, pruning all the rosebushes and other plants. The garage was a mess, and I cleaned it out also. In fact, there was so much debris that my husband Richard rented a dumpster to be placed in front of our house.

After ten days of cleaning, I was tired, but glad to have all that work behind me. I was looking forward to the weekend. The following morning, I showered, dressed, and made out a "to-do" list for the day. My morning was running normally. I had all the ceiling fans on and was listening to my stereo. Our basset hounds, Morgan and Bud, were lying on the cool deck by the pool, and our other dog, Belle, was in the serenity garden.

Soon, things would become anything but serene!

As I sat at the breakfast bar, I decided to look in the dining room hutch and buffet to make sure there was nothing more I wanted to throw away. Inside the buffet, I found an old Ouija board, still in its original box. I had owned it for so many years, I could not remember where it had come from. I decided to take it out of the box and place it on the kitchen table. I placed my hands on the planchette and asked aloud, "Is anybody there?"

I must admit, I giggled to myself, thinking it was just a silly board game. I asked two more times, "Is anybody there?"

The planchette moved, and spelled out "J-O-N." Suddenly things weren't so funny anymore.

The planchette continued to move, with "Jon" spelling out vile words, and expressing anger. He then spelled out: "CAN'T SEE. CAN'T SEE. HA HA HA."

I immediately released the planchette. I was nervous. I placed the board back in the box, and put it in the drawer.

At that moment, Morgan and Bud started howling. Belle started pacing back and forth on the patio. She was a nervous wreck. The stereo stopped playing, although the ceiling fans continued to turn.

Moments later the dogs got sick and began to throw up uncontrollably. I felt that I was going to be sick also, but the feeling passed.

I sat out in my garden, watching my dogs act so strangely. They wouldn't come to me at all. I prayed, "Sweet Jesus, what have I done?"

Later in the afternoon, things seemed to have settled down. However, the worst was yet to come. That evening, after dinner, I told my husband what had happened. He laughed and said, "It's just a board game."

I asked, "I wonder what 'can't see, can't see' means?" Richard shrugged his shoulders over the whole ordeal.

Later that evening, I was in the living room, writing letters. All of a sudden, I heard Belle crying out. I ran into the spare bedroom where she slept and turned the light on. She looked so frightened. Her ears were straight back and her tail was tucked under her body. She kept crying and I couldn't touch her without her crying out more. I finally coaxed her into the living room with me. She would not go back to that bedroom.

The next morning, I awoke feeling as though there was a pillow on my face. I swiped at the phantom pillow, and realized that I could not see. My right eye was swollen shut! I had been bitten by a spider on my eyelid right where my eyelashes were. For three days, my lid stayed closed. After three weeks, my eyelid healed and I could see fine.

The dogs were still exhibiting strange behavior. They would bark and growl for no apparent reason. I was having trouble concentrating on my studies. Things in the house began to fall apart. The air conditioner broke down and we had to have the motor replaced. Our clothes dryer needed a new motor. Both bathroom commodes broke—one had to be replaced. Three garden hoses exploded and had to be replaced. The grave of a baby basset hound we had lost two years previously was desecrated.

Before the city removed the dumpster, I took the Ouija board and threw it in the container. The day the city came to remove the dumpster I stood at my kitchen window and watched as they loaded it on a truck and drove away. I went outside and checked on the ground to make sure that the evil board was gone.

I know many of you think of a Ouija board as a silly game, and so did I. But now I have a different perspective on the evil that can come about from a game created for the fun of children.

—Dolly Smith, Tulare, California
March 2000

The Ouija Board

After the terrible attack on Pearl Harbor in 1941, President Roosevelt announced that the United States was at WAR! Our male and female friends and relatives volunteered or were drafted to serve in the Army, Navy, Marines, and Air Forces. Of course, this was a sad and often tragic time for those who remained at home.

As the long war went on, our thoughts were with our loved ones so far away. They were not permitted to let us know where they were stationed. Suddenly, a board game, known as Ouija, became very popular. The board had the letters of the alphabet arranged in a semicircle, with the words "Yes" and "No" in the corners; another corner had a question mark. The board came with a three-legged pointer.

One day, my friend Sally invited me and two others

for dinner. After dinner, she brought out her Ouija board. Her intention was to ask the board where her husband Frank was located. Sally and our two friends placed their hands on the board. I was elected to write anything that might come through.

The pointer would only work for Sally. Our two friends gave up, accusing Sally of having fun with us and moving the pointer herself. Her feelings were hurt.

"If you think I am doing it, blindfold me and let's see what happens! I just have to know where Frank is," Sally protested. We took her up on the idea and blindfolded her securely. The pointer raced from letter to letter. She asked for Frank's location. It spelled out "ALDERSHOT, ENGLAND." Then I had an idea. In my purse was a snapshot of a friend who had died recently. I placed it on the board. Sally was still blindfolded. While we watched it, it spelled "PICTURE OF MAN IN HEAVEN." On that note, we ended the session, with eerie feelings.

I wish I could say that was the end of it, but it was not. A few days later, I had a phone call from Sally. She was frightened! Ever since she played the Ouija board, strange things were happening in her home: lights going on and off, weird shadows, and then, worst of all, a terrifying apparition. Sally heard her baby screaming in the next room, and ran to see what was wrong. There was a white figure bent over the baby! The figure turned and looked at her, then disappeared! That very night, she chopped up that Ouija board and threw it in the furnace. This seemed to end the haunting.

My story does not end there. Frank returned home wounded, and was awarded the Purple Heart. Sally and all of us learned that, indeed, at the very time we played the Ouija board, Frank had been stationed at Aldershot, England!

—Adria Gillis, Long Beach, California
December 1999

Taps for the Captain

Fort Fred Steele, Wyoming, was built to protect the Union Pacific Railroad construction crews from hostile Indians when they were building a bridge across the North Platte River.

In 1955, my family moved from Greeley, Colorado to Fort Steele. My father had purchased the old officer's quarters for $800—a four-plex house that had 16 rooms.

It had a beautiful double stairway and solid oak banisters. Halfway up the left-hand banister, we noticed a deep gash in the wood. Legend had it that the commanding officer had drawn his saber and slammed it into the banister upon learning of the death of his son, who had been on patrol for hostile Indians.

Due to Fort Steele's remote location, most of my time was spent practicing my trumpet, and it was this that brought me my closest contact with the captain.

I had gone to bed after an evening of practice and was awakened by a feeling of warmth and love. As I looked toward the door of my room, I saw the captain standing there looking at me, seemingly with a tear running down his cheek. He approached the side of my bed and laid his hand on my horn case. Suddenly I thought I knew what he wanted. I got up, picked up my horn and, facing the parade ground, I blew taps.

The captain stood at attention, appeared to salute me, and faded away. We never saw him again, but when I think of him, I recall the love and caring I felt that night so long ago.

—Steve Brundy, St. Paul, Minnesota
October 1993

Grave Robber

Several years ago I did a lot of traveling. I design custom jewelry and cut stones and would sell them at gem and jewelry shows. At a show in 1982, I was walking around looking at the displays. I ran across a case filled with Native American items on display, though they were not for sale.

I felt a presence next to me and turned to find a

man in his forties wearing an Indian-style jacket and a cowboy hat with feathers and beadwork. He looked at me for a moment.

"I know this may sound strange," he said, "but I was told to talk to you and that you could help me."

Knowing several people at the show, I thought he had come to see me about jewelry design. Boy, was I wrong! I asked who had sent him, but he just looked at the floor and said, "I was told you would know what had happened to me and what to do about it."

I'm not sure how I knew, but I sensed it wasn't a "someone" who had sent him to me.

"All right," I said, hesitating. "I'll try."

His name was Billy. He was half Native American, and he collected arrowheads, pots, buckskin clothes, and other artifacts, which he displayed in a room in his house. He was self-employed and married, and life had been good to him until about six months prior to our conversation.

His uncle, who owned a large ranch, called one day to tell him a road construction crew had uncovered what appeared to be the remains of an old Indian camp. He said there were pots (mostly broken), arrowheads, and several other items.

Billy said he broke all speed records getting down to the ranch the following day to meet his uncle. The area wasn't large, but there were several broken pots on the ground. Then he saw what his uncle had meant by "other items"—bones. Billy had always said he would not touch a grave, and the site looked like a burial ground to him.

They were still looking around the area when Billy heard a voice. "I would love to have a skull," it said. His uncle looked at him out of the corner of his eye, but told him to take his pick—there were several around. Billy swore to me that he had not spoken. He said his body moved as if in a dream. He picked up several items, including a skull, placed them in a cardboard box, and put them in his truck.

It was quite late when Billy got home that night. He left the box in his truck and went to bed. He forgot about the box until he was leaving the next morning and saw it in his truck. He put it in his house, and that night he cleaned the contents and put them in a display case.

That was when the trouble began. Billy's health began to slip. His work began to fall off. His truck mysteriously caught fire—twice in one day. He began to have trouble at home. He broke his leg. He had several nightmares about the skull.

Billy decided his luck might change if he got rid of the relics. He took the items to a woman he knew who was in charge of an exhibition of Native American artifacts. He told her about his troubles and asked her if she would take the skull. She agreed, but said it wouldn't solve his problems. She was right. His health grew worse. He went in and out of hospitals, but no one could figure out what was wrong with him.

The weekend of our conversation, Billy felt better and had come to the jewelry show. He said he had been about to leave when he saw me and knew he had to speak to me.

I had never met Billy or his uncle, but as he was telling me his story, I started to see the places he was talking about as though I knew the area. I began to describe the layout of the land. As I spoke, I could see his face turn white. He asked when I had been to the ranch. I assured him I had never been there.

When I told him that the skull he had taken hadn't been with the other bones, but had been on a small rise to his right all by itself, he took a step back, his eyes widening. He took a deep breath and asked, almost in a whisper, "How did you know, if you weren't there?" I told him I wasn't sure, but that it was as clear as a photo in my head.

He asked me why he had taken the skull when he had never wanted one before. I heard the answer in my head and told him he was meant to have it, but that he didn't need to be told what he had done wrong. I could see the tears in his eyes. He knew that he had grabbed the skull and run, just like a grave robber.

We talked for a while. He asked me what he could do to be forgiven. I told him he had to find his own answer to that, but I was confident he would.

I eventually heard from Billy again. He had retrieved the skull, returned it to the Earth, and prayed for forgiveness. Since then his illness had been diagnosed, his business had picked up, and he and his wife were getting along much better. He knew he had been forgiven.

As for me, when someone says "I was told to talk to you," I just look inward and ask for the help to come as it will.

—Wes Simmonds, Gladewater, Texas
July 1998

Laura, the Friendly Ghost

In 1971, I was dating Chris St. John, a man who lived in one of the older neighborhoods of Kansas City in a house he had bought from his parents, who had moved to a farm.

One night we were sitting on the sofa in his living room, facing the dining room. The two rooms were connected by a wide-open doorway. Suddenly I saw a woman standing in it. She was pale, with white-blonde hair, and she was dressed in an old-fashioned, lacy-white dress. She looked so solid and three-dimensional that I could have sworn a person was standing there, looking at me. But then she faded into nothing and I found myself wondering if I'd imagined everything.

I told Chris shakily that I thought someone was in the dining room, but he responded that I had seen the dog.

I shook my head so emphatically that he became intrigued. "What did the person look like?" he asked. When I described her, he said, "You just saw Laura."

He immediately jumped up and called his mother, who told him, "I was wondering when she was going to make an appearance. She usually shows up about this time of year."

As soon as I found out that Laura was a ghost, all the color must have drained out of my face, because Chris told me not to worry, that she was friendly. He didn't know her story, but apparently everyone in his family was well acquainted with her. Since then I've always believed in ghosts. As they say, seeing is believing.

—Celeste White, Redding, California
January 1995

Norman's House

In 1981 my husband and I bought a lovely cottage from a recently widowed woman. She and her husband had built the home in 1932 and added rooms through the years. The one-acre lot was beautifully landscaped, and our three children loved to play among the flowers, mazes, and statuary.

The widow's son, Norman, was distraught over the sale of his childhood home. I was so happy about owning this beautiful home that when I heard he died of cancer in 1985, I gave only a passing thought to that sullen, lonely man.

I began having strange accidents around the home and terrible nightmares that increased in intensity. The message clearly said to me, "Get out!" When my dreams showed the home filling with snakes that chased me and my children, threatening our lives, I began to cry all the time. My husband and friends thought I was having a nervous breakdown. Finally, because I feared for my children, we sold the home I loved so much.

We purchased another home in the same town. I drove by our old house, watching as four different families moved in from 1986 to 1992. All left within a year, distraught and depressed. I heard stories of failed marriages, attempted suicide, and financial difficulties that plagued them. The most startling news came from a realtor who said the house was full of snakes at one showing.

The house was repossessed by the bank. During the year and a half it was empty, neighbors sometimes saw a light on in the second-floor bedroom. In January 1994 another family moved in. I pray that all the snakes are gone.

—Kathleen Z. Eames, Charlestown, New Hampshire
February 1995

Phantom Clipper Ship

In July 1959 I was sailing on the Belgian Line freighter *Lufira* out of New York bound to Matadi, port of entry for the (then) Belgian Congo. The ship carried 12 passengers, most of them missionary families. The 22-day voyage included stops at Dakar, Monrovia, Freetown, Lagos, and Lome. On the 17th of July we crossed the equator and I was initiated with the baptism of Neptune. Sometime after midnight that same night we ran into a sudden storm and the ship began to rock with the waves.

I left my cabin and went out on deck to watch the majestic angry Atlantic. Amidst heavy rain, waves were pounding the deck to the background of thunder and lightning. While I stood holding the rail a sudden burst of lightning illuminated the waves on the port side of the freighter and drew my attention to another ship about 200 feet away.

What startled me was that the other vessel was a sailing ship. At first I took it to be a private yacht but as I gazed at it amid the rising waves I realized it resembled a clipper ship of the last century. It had three masts and five rows of sails; the bottom sail in front was torn and flapping in the wind. For a brief moment when it seemed to draw closer I could see men climbing the mast. The lightning continued and I stared at the sailing ship in amazement for about 10 minutes. Suddenly I felt a sense of fear as I realized I was entirely alone on the stormy deck.

I returned below to my cabin to fetch my camera and awakened a fellow passenger—John Dobry, an oil engineer—to come topside with me to view the strange ship. But by the time we had returned to the top deck the lightning had ceased and the clipper ship was nowhere to be seen. Dobry accused me of having been drinking or dreaming but I assured him I was wide awake and sober the whole time.

The following day I asked the captain about the sailing ship and he likewise accused me of dreaming. None of the other passengers had seen the vessel nor could the crew supply any information. Two days later we landed at Matadi. As I was about to debark, an English sailor who worked in the galley confirmed what I had seen and told me it was a "ghost ship." My own theory is that somehow the unusual atmosphere created by the intense electrical storm tuned us into a wavelength from the past and that in 1959 I somehow gazed upon a ship from the 1860s.

—Thomas Spelios, Fort Lee, New Jersey
April 1973

Hands from the Holocaust

Midway through a visit to Poland, my companion Wanda and I took an early train from Krakow to a city known better for its name than its environs. It is a city of 40,000 people, most of whom are employed by one of the mines or industries whose smog blankets the area. Its name, in Polish, is Oswiecim, and beside it is the small village of Brzezinka, or Auschwitz-Birkenau, site of World War II's most infamous concentration camp, which we planned to visit.

After a two-mile walk from the railway station, we came to an ominous brick and barbed-wire gate. It was open. We stepped inside, where several other groups of tourists were wandering the camp, which has been left largely as it was found by the troops who liberated it in 1945. There was no sound but the wind. Barbed-wire encloses more than a square mile at Birkenau, and a square mile can hold a lot of silence.

Beyond crumbling barracks and rusting barbed wire, one modern concession has been made to the memory of the 1.5 million who died in Birkenau. An ugly, misshapen monument stands between the ruins of two gas chamber crematorium complexes blown up by retreating Germans. We wanted to see the monument and began the one-and-a-half mile walk across the camp.

Our route followed rusting rail lines that once led to the gas chambers. We walked past rickety wooden watchtowers and past the ramp where SS officers once stood to dispense life or death with a wave of a white-gloved hand.

The air seemed thicker and more difficult to walk through about 100 yards from the monument. The sensation increased in strength until I felt like I was walking into a taut, thin rubber sheet that was holding me back. My ears felt as though they had absorbed a sound of great volume, almost as if they were ringing from an explosion. Beyond the boundaries of the camp I could hear crowing roosters, barking dogs, and distant traffic. But nearby, there was nothing. Nothing but that eerie sensation.

I turned to Wanda, intending to say that the atmosphere of the place was getting to me. The words died in my throat as she turned to me. "I don't like this," she said in a small voice. "It feels like someone is pushing me."

The hair rose on my neck and suddenly the strange sensation made sense. We were being warned and physically and spiritually pushed away from the spot we were approaching, the killing ground where many of the one-and-a-half million had perished.

We lingered briefly at the monument while invisible hands pushed at us and silent voices trembled in my ears. Although we had planned to spend the day exploring the camp, we had no desire to linger. The sensation of being warned faded as we turned our backs to the monument, but as we wandered through a few of the barracks and along the once-electrified fence, we still felt hurried and uneasy. The feeling persisted until we passed out the gate and left that evil place behind.

The day was windy, with low clouds and bursts of rain. For the remainder of my journey, I tried to convince myself that what Wanda and I had experienced was merely the result of a suggestive atmosphere affecting two vivid imaginations. Several weeks later, however, I would reconsider.

During my travels I took hundreds of photos. My 12-year-old camera was very reliable. All of the 700 photos I took during the trip turned out perfectly, except for one series of exposures.

The photos I took inside Auschwitz-Birkenau were, with one exception, badly underexposed. Images taken outside the camp immediately before and after my visit were flawless. Lighting conditions had not changed during that time, and the camera's meter had been set on automatic. Yet of more than 24 photos, only a single view of the monument was properly exposed, as if I were permitted a single souvenir of my visit.

I have been a lifelong skeptic with regard to otherworldly things, but I now believe I have been to a haunted place. Its ghosts sought to warn me away from a place they knew as a site of unimaginable horror and death, a place of such spiritual darkness that even light, as evidenced by my ruined film, did not behave as it should. I shall heed their wishes, for I shall never return.

—Peter MacKenzie, Hibbing, Minnesota
September 1995

Strange Indeed

There are more things in heaven and earth, Horatio, than are dreamt of in your philosophy, said Shakespeare's Hamlet. The stories in this chapter are not easily categorized. Perhaps someday experiences such as these will be explained by the laws of modern science. Until that day, read on, and remember that many people have experienced strange things here on earth that are undreamt of in scientific theory.

Miracle of the Picture

At five o'clock on the morning of July 24, 1947, I woke strangling and choking in my room. Black and heavy smoke filled the house.

Struggling into consciousness, I sprang from the bed and fought my way into the hall. Smoke turned me back into another passage. I plunged down the stairs and finally reached an outer door that was locked and barred for protection. With trembling fingers I finally loosened the heavy chains, flung the door open, and dashed into the outer air.

My Cape Cod home was ablaze and burning fiercely.

For hours the fire raged—long tongues of flame reaching out into the garden, even to the studio and the garage. Even the fine old shade trees did not escape. At 4 P.M., the fire having raged since five that morning, the Fire Chief came to me and said sympathetically, "It is a total loss."

I had rushed from the building in a cotton nightdress and bare feet. That was all I had with which to begin life over again.

The loss was so appalling, so overwhelming, I did not remember individual treasures until later.

On my desk in the living room a tiny picture of my mother was always before me when I sat there to work. Some months later a particular need arose for my mother's picture. Sorrowfully I realized that nothing had been saved from that room. The picture was irretrievably gone.

Having learned by long years of effort to overcome many handicaps, there seemed absolutely nothing I could do in this case. My heart was heavy with my loss.

Months later, back in my New York home, I needed something from a little-used chest drawer. Turning over some handkerchiefs, I saw the well-known frame, face down. I hardly had strength to lift the tiny thing. It was the same picture which, on the morning of the fire, had rested on my desk in the Cape Cod house. It was perfect, without mar or blemish.

—Dr. Ellaine Elmore
March 1950

Lost and Found

I love flea markets, yard sales, and rummage sales. I look for unusual objects, not antiques or valuables. The item has to appeal to me.

About a year ago, I purchased a knife at a flea market in Clanton, Alabama. It is an old knife. The leather case is very worn and scratched. I really didn't look at the knife very closely except to notice that it would be nice to use at the barn or while walking in the woods. When I brought it home, I put it with a stack of other things that I had purchased the same way over the years.

Since I am selling my mobile home, I have been packing up all the junk that I have collected over the years. I am storing it all at my parents' house for a while. As I walked onto the porch, I showed the knife to my father. He asked to look at it more closely. I carried the rest of the things that I had into the house. When I came back out, my father pointed out the scratching on the knife case. I could see clearly the initials "PDH." I know that they had already been there—he did not scratch them in. I remember seeing the scratches, I just hadn't looked closely at them. Also, he is a very honest person and would not invent this story.

In 1940, he had been in the army at Fort Knox, Kentucky. He was deaf in one ear but got in by not telling about it. He was issued the knife along with other items that he stored in a locker by his bed. When they found out that he couldn't hear, they sent him to a hospital for a check-up. He begged to stay in, even if it meant kitchen duty, but they sent him straight home from the hospital with an honorable (medical) discharge. He never received the things in his locker; they were stolen and never recovered—until now.

His knife showed up at a flea market sometime in 1998. His daughter bought it and brought it home to him.

—Carol Headley, Deatsville, Alabama
May 2000

A Good Luck Gold Charm

In October 1976 my husband died, ten days before my birthday. However, he had had my daughter purchase a gold charm in the shape of a horn, an Italian good luck symbol, as my birthday gift. I wore this constantly.

One day in March of 1982 it had snowed heavily in New York. On my way home from work I stopped off to do some shopping. After parking my car, I carried my packages up to my apartment and after putting the groceries away, I noticed the charm had fallen off the chain on which I wore it. I immediately retraced my steps, checked out my car, and then went back and forth over the route I had taken (four or five times in the snow) but to no avail. I was heartsick!

That night I felt "something" being put in the palm of my hand. Half asleep I remember closing my hand around "something" and putting it on the nightstand next to my bed and then falling back asleep.

When I awoke the next morning there was the charm on the nightstand next to my bed.

—Frances Ricard, Corfton, Maryland
February 1992

Heart of the Forest

Most of the woods in Firecrest, Washington, the area where I grew up, had been cleared for development, but thanks to a loophole in the law, the sprawling forest across the street had been spared. As a child I felt a special connection to this ancient place and would spend endless hours in the playground of its massive, moss-covered trees.

Once in 1984 when I was home from Gonzaga University on Spokane, Washington, for the weekend, I felt an irresistible urge to go to the forest. It had been years since I'd been there, but I felt a call I could not resist.

I started into the heart of the forest with a purpose I could not explain. As a kid, I had wandered aimlessly in this maze of trails, but not now. I passed two kids on the trail, snickering over something they had done, but I had a nameless destination to reach and barely noticed them.

After walking for a good 15 minutes and choosing between many different trails, I suddenly came across an old, dead tree stump alight with flames.

This fire had been lit by the kids I had passed on the trail, I realized, and I knew that if I hadn't found it, eventually the whole forest would have caught on fire. Fetching water from the nearby pond, I doused these unnatural flames.

I don't know if my stumbling upon the fire was just an incredible coincidence, but to this day, I believe that the forest—a consciousness of the trees and plants—called to me to rescue it.

I don't know if the trees called me in particular or if I was simply the only one who heard their call, but I do know that I now treat all forests with even more respect than I did before.

—Brent Hartinger, Seattle, Washington
November 1993

Carolina Monster Meets U.S. Marines

I have been a subscriber to *FATE Magazine* for many years, and feel that this experience will be of interest to other *FATE* readers. In March of 1958, I was stationed at Camp Lejeune, North Carolina, in the United States Marine Corps, having just returned from two years of duty in Okinawa, Japan. Two Marine buddies and I decided to take a trip to Myrtle Beach, South Carolina. Having little money between us and no transportation of our own, we decided to try hitchhiking. We started out on a Friday morning with a 72-hour pass.

After about 10 hours of different rides, we finally got out of North Carolina and into South Carolina. When it became dark, the rides dried up. After walking about 10 miles, we decided to call it a night and spotted some picnic benches off to the side of the road near a clearing in the woods. We decided that this was where we were going to spend the night and sleep on the benches. I slept on the bench closest to the woods. The three of us went right to sleep, knowing that the next morning we would stand a better chance to hitch a ride. As you can well imagine, it wasn't exactly like a mattress, but we all finally got to sleep.

At approximately 5:30 A.M., it began to get light and I was the first one awake. Well, you can just imagine my shock—while rubbing my eyes, I looked into the woods and saw this large creature, about six or seven feet tall with long brown hair and fiery red eyes just staring at me. The creature began walking toward us. After what seemed like an eternity, I jumped up and began yelling. There we were—three brave Marines running for their lives. All three of us had been in firefights and were not easily rattled.

It's been more than 40 years since this happened, and I still think of it as if it was yesterday. Believe me, it wasn't a bear or any familiar animal. We all agreed it was something none of us had ever seen before.

Incidentally, we never did make it to Myrtle Beach.

—Kenneth Synnot, Las Vegas, Nevada
November 2000

The Unholy Highball

In the fall of 1994, I was completing my last year as a student at St. Olaf College in Northfield, Minnesota. Life was good. I lived in a funky little apartment, a stone's throw from the Cannon River and about a mile and a half from campus. The supermarket across the street was open all night, presumably for the convenience of third-shift employees of Northfield's Malt-O-Meal factory but also quite convenient for study breaks and late-night snack runs. I did most of my grocery shopping after midnight. This convenience, and more importantly, the apartment's strategic position outside the enforcement zone of St. Olaf's draconian beverage regulations, made me the natural host for many an enjoyable weekend event. The most supernaturally memorable of these occurred on Halloween of that year.

Midterm exams had just been completed, and the assembled guests were in high spirits, releasing the tensions of student life in low-tech amusements such as vintage Atari video-game competitions, and the hurling of pumpkins into the river. These activities were fueled by generous quantities of Hamm's golden ale, but what happened at midnight cannot be explained away as a boozy delusion.

As the Witching Hour approached, I found myself in charge of a spontaneous cookie-baking operation in my apartment's tiny kitchen. Suddenly, our mixing was interrupted by a sharp crash and a rain of shiny fragments.

Investigating the mysterious debris, I recognized the shattered remains of a heavy cocktail glass that had been sitting empty on the countertop just moments before. From the distribution of the shards, it appeared as if this glass had been caused to burst apart by forces unknown. It clearly had not fallen to the floor, or otherwise been moved from its location; furthermore, it was not exposed to any source of heat or vibration which might explain its sudden and violent disintegration.

One completely sober witness (the designated driver for about two dozen of the people present, God bless her) asserted later that she had watched the glass shatter from across the apartment. She saw a flash of light above the glass just prior to the anomalous explosion.

The exploding glass was my only experience with poltergeist-type activity in that apartment. Looking back, I feel this singular outburst may have had some connection with a highly-charged romantic situation involving certain individuals present that night, but of course there is no way of confirming that possibility.

—Andrew Honigman, Minneapolis, Minnesota
January 2000

The Key Ring

Have you ever wanted something so badly you could almost reach out and touch your mental image of it? All of us long for things, and I'm no exception. This time, I wanted a key ring.

Perhaps the desire for a key ring seems mundane, but I simply had to have one. Not just any key ring, either. I needed a large, metallic disk inscribed with Piscean symbolism.

One day I set out to find this talisman. With high hopes I ventured into the shops of downtown Denver. But after hours of darting in and out of doorways, I hadn't found anything close.

I thought this was ridiculous. Someone must have had it.

After spending all day walking and searching, I finally gave up. As I trudged back to my apartment, I noticed a van parked in front of the building. A man I didn't recognize stood by the driver's side door.

"Gloria," he called. "I don't think you remember me, but we've met at the restaurant where you work. I've been waiting here hoping you'd show up. I've got something for you, something I think you should have. Don't know why. Hold on."

He reached into his van and brought a flat, yellowish object out in his hand. "This is for you."

When the gift was in my hands, I freaked out, for it was a key ring. The ring was brass, and of unique design. I held it closer. My hands began to tremble. It was Piscean.

"How in the world?" I said, and told him the story of my search.

"I've been sorting through my stuff, getting ready to move," he explained, "and when I saw this old key ring, I suddenly realized it was meant for you."

Then he said goodbye, climbed into his van, and drove away. I never saw him again.

After 17 years of constant use, my key ring is worn and thin. Still, I cherish it. It is a treasure, a reminder to me of how yearnings for the simplest of things may be fulfilled in unusual ways. Goddess does provide in unexpected, fun ways.

—Gloria Montgomery, Silverthorne, Colorado
April 1994

George's Truck Miracle

My friend George was a party man and a womanizer. He was going through his second divorce and his fourth or fifth job in two years. He had to sell his boat when it broke loose from its mooring one night and rammed another boat. Then he lost his job because of his party lifestyle, and things were looking grim.

With the little money he had left, he purchased a secondhand truck to use for hauling small loads. He hoped to make enough money from this to eventually open a small moving company. The second day into this venture was when the "truck miracle" occurred.

The truck was loaded with heavy items. As he crossed a railroad track, the truck's rear wheel sank into a deep pothole between the tracks. The truck came to a stop and died. Nothing he did would bring it back to life. In desperation he tried levering the truck out of the pothole with a two-by-four. No luck. Then the crossing bell sounded. A train was coming. Looking down the track, George saw the freight train approaching. His business was about to end in its infancy.

Walking off the track so he wouldn't be injured in the collision, George said aloud, "God, please help me. Please, please help me."

No sooner did he utter this plea than the truck lifted itself out of the pothole and rolled safely off the track, out of the path of the oncoming train. The truck still would not start, but it was safe.

George no longer drinks, and he has dedicated his life to his church and to helping others in distress. He has a good job that he has held for four years. The truck miracle has changed his life completely.

—Charles W. Rockett, San Marcos, California
August 1998

Lighter Than Air

I have worked at a nursing home for many years, and unfortunately, I have seen many patients take their last breaths. One particular incident was of a very strange nature that no one to this day can explain.

One of our patients, who was very religious, was dying, and we expected her to leave this world at any time. She was a solidly built person weighing approximately 150 pounds. This patient had suffered several strokes, and she was almost paralyzed on both sides. It took two nurse's aides to attend to her daily needs.

Several minutes after she was pronounced dead, one of the nurse's aides went into the room to prepare her body before it was to be picked up by the funeral home. Expecting that it would take two people to help with the preparation, the aide asked for assistance. When the two aides started to move the patient's body, they found that she was as light as a feather. The aides were shocked—it was as though the dead woman's spirit had gone straight to heaven. It had somehow been magically lifted up, and it had left an empty shell behind.

The nurse's aides later told the rest of the staff what had happened. We concluded that all of the prayers from loved ones had helped to release her soul from its body.

This is a story that we'll never forget, and that we have talked about ever since.

—Linda Haluska, Willow Springs, Illinois
February 1996

The Lechusa

When I was ten years old, I was living with my grandparents from my dad's side. My dad was a truck driver at the time and had invited me to go with him on a trip to Laredo. He was transporting melons and wanted to start the drive early, so we left around two o'clock in the morning. I can still remember; it was cool and very dark, aside from the glow of the moon. We were traveling at a speed of 55 to 70 miles per hour. My dad wanted to reach our destination before sunrise.

All of a sudden, the passenger-side door opened where I was sitting. To my surprise, I saw an old lady standing on the side step, holding the door open and beckoning me with her finger to go with her. I turned to look at my dad in silence.

My dad said, "Give me your hand, and close the door." I guess he didn't want to stop.

I turned back to the lady, but she was gone. Yet the door was still wide open, regardless of the air pressure from the speed we were driving. I snapped out of the shock I was in when my dad grabbed my wrist, so I could close the door.

After a while I asked him if he had seen the lady holding the door open. He just looked at me sideways, with an eyebrow raised, for a few seconds. At just that instant, we saw a lady standing in the middle of the road, right in front of the truck. Too late to brake—we hit her.

My dad stopped the truck, and we got out to look. There was no blood on the truck's grille, just white feathers from a large bird. My dad said that it was a *lechusa*—a "witch owl" that people turn into.

We didn't bother to go back to check the road, nor did he report the incident. He then explained to me about these *lechusas* that are common in Texas. I never told my dad that she was the same lady holding the door open to the truck.

Was death calling me at a young age, or was it some message from the dead?

—Efrain Yanez, Donna, Texas
May 2000

A Blessed Sighting

On a Wednesday evening in 1968, I went to a special mass at St. Lawrence O'Toole in Oakland, California, for the showing of the statue of the Lady of Lourdes. At the time, I was ten years old. My mother, Cecilia Wood, had been the organist for quite a few years. I was the first baby ever baptized at the opening of the new church in 1957. I had been a patient at Shriner's Children's Hospital in San Francisco for the treatment of a brittle bone disease called osteogenese imperfecta, which I had had since birth. One characteristic of this disease is that the spine is dwarfed and all the bones are severely brittle. At ten years of age, I was all legs, with a very short spine; x-rays showed that my spine was only ten inches long. Doctors at Shriner's told my parents and me that the disease was a condition I had to live with.

The congregation at St. Lawrence O'Toole wrote prayers and placed them in a box. Later, a few of the prayers would be chosen by the priest to be read aloud during mass. I wrote my special prayer asking everyone to pray that my spine would grow. From the hundreds of prayers in the box, the priest chose mine.

At the end of the service, everyone got in line to give their thanks to the healing saint, the Lady of Lourdes. When it was my turn, I knelt before the statue, and when I looked up to kiss her feet, I saw that she had become alive. The statue's eyes were painted blue, but now her eyes appeared dark brown and her hands seemed to reach out and touch my head. I began to cry, but I was not scared. I could only tell my mother that the lady was alive and that she had touched me. Whether what happened was just my child's imagination or not, I cannot tell. I only know that the experience had been real for me, and to this day I can still feel her hands on my head.

When I went for my regular checkup at Shriner's, x-rays were taken of my spine. The doctors were dumbfounded; in the two months since my last visit, my spine had grown three inches. Everyone looked on in amazement. I only smiled, because I knew the truth, and to this day I still believe in faith and the power of prayer.

—Gretchen Wood, Hyampom, California
January 1996

Witch's Grave

One of the strangest occurrences of my life happened in north-central Kentucky on October 17, 1976. That month newspaper reporter Bryan Wooley of the Louisville *Courier-Journal* wrote a story about the only known execution of a witch in Kentucky. It had occurred in 1823, but he had been unable to find out where the remains of the witch were buried. So in his article he asked anyone who knew the location of her grave to contact him. At the time I read his story I had no idea when the woman had died or even what her name was.

A short time later I was hiking with four other men along a ridge above the Ohio River, in the area Wooley had written about, when we came upon the foundation of a house almost completely hidden in the woods. The others walked on but I decided to check out the remains of this old dwelling. The usual debris of an abandoned country home was scattered about. I learned later no one had lived on this old farm for 60 or 70 years. It was quiet and lonely; the only sounds were the cackling of hens in a distant farmyard, the far-off barking of a dog, and the song of a meadowlark on the wind.

Standing there alone, I noticed an overgrown lane that led off down a small hill where it lost itself in the woods. Knowing the other men would wait for me farther on, I decided to follow this long-forgotten path.

I had walked several hundred yards down the hill when I noticed a clump of wild rosebushes a short distance from the path. They seemed out of place here in the woods. Pushing my way toward them, I came upon a rough gravestone. It was lying flat on the ground, almost covered with leaves and dirt, at the head of a slight depression such as a sunken old grave might make. The gravestone obviously had weathered many a season.

Cleaning away the debris, I saw that it had carved on it, in a beautiful script, the name Elizabeth Tincheor, 1799–1823. Directly beneath the name and dates were these words, "Suffer not a witch to live."

No roots of the rosebushes had grown under or around the old tombstone as would be normal in a thicket. Rather, it seemed the flowers were bent over it in an attempt to conceal the marker from prying eyes. I cannot explain what led me to it but I do recall noticing as I stood beside it that it was one of the most beautiful autumn days I had ever seen, October 17, 1976. Since Elizabeth Tincheor, age 24, had been laid to rest here and someone had planted the roses, 153 years had passed.

After photographing it, I pushed the rosebushes together, hiding it again from prying eyes.

Only after I returned home did I remember the story I had read a few days before about a witch having been executed in the area I had just visited. Calling the newspaper reporter, I asked him the witch's name, when she was executed and what her age had been.

He replied, "Elizabeth Tincheor, October 17, 1823. She was 24 years old."

Somehow I wasn't surprised.

The reporter was extremely anxious to learn the location of the grave so that he could do a follow-up story with photographs, but somehow I could not bring myself to tell him where it was. I guess I felt that while she had lived, Elizabeth Tincheor had known too much of life's bitterness and too little of its kindness. Her secret resting place among the wild roses remains safe with me.

After talking with the reporter, I realized I had come upon her grave exactly 153 years to the day after she was executed.

—Michael Paul Henson, Jeffersonville, Indiana
June 1984

Special Delivery

In July 1957 I ordered a set of books that I thought might help me in various puzzle contests. About a week later when a medium-sized carton arrived addressed to our house, but with no name or return address on it, I concluded that it must be my set of books.

No one else was expecting any package so I eagerly carried it up to my room and excitedly tore it open. I was dismayed at what confronted me. It was not my set of books but about six small rows of printed cards, all italicized, presumably to be filled in by some religious organization upon the death of one of its members.

Puzzled and annoyed at this mean turn of events I tried to collect my thoughts as to the best procedure to follow in order to locate its proper owner.

Suddenly I was seized by a strong, compelling urge "to hurry up and look at those crumpled pieces of newspapers surrounding the cards!"

This, I decided, was utter nonsense. I stubbornly refused to yield to this idiotic premonition but again I was silently, forcefully commanded "open up those newspapers, you fool!"

Hesitantly, I followed this fantastic premonition and opened first one torn, crumpled piece of newspaper and then another. Upon opening the third piece of newspaper I saw that it was part of a New York daily printed just two days before. A black-bordered obituary column seemed to shriek up at me!

As I glanced down the list of names, right in the center of the page my eyes became riveted on the death announcement of my sister's husband.

This sister, confined in an institution for many years, had been released only a few weeks before. Due to circumstances beyond our control we had lost contact with her husband and his family who had thought it best to exclude themselves from contact with us although they had been rearing my sister's only child since birth.

My two other sisters and I discussed this new knowledge. By calling up the funeral parlor we learned that my sister's husband had died of a heart attack in a candy store. Knowing he was a veteran of World War II, we contacted the Veteran's Administration and now my sister has some share of the comforts which his pension brings.

If I had not been compelled, by unknown forces, to smooth out packing papers she most certainly would have been deprived of this money that she desperately needs.

Not many days after this unusual occurrence a woman rang our doorbell and inquired about a lost package. She explained it had been inadvertently addressed to our street and it just happened that our house number corresponded to hers.

She went away with her package—which had told us something we needed to know.

—Olga Jaros, Elmhurst, New York
November 1960

The Crucifix

A narrow path wound down a hill designated as Hill 340 on Sergeant Tomlinson's map, a small part of the hellish real estate known as Korea. The trail then led along a frozen ditch at the foot of yet another rise, number 420 on the map, which rose sharply 300 yards off to the right across a valley.

The patrol had been uneventful. Its recognizance failed to locate the enemy positions that General Headquarters had reported were in the area.

Sergeant Tomlinson tapped the man in front of him on the shoulder. "In the ditch; pass the word."

The men scrambled into the comforting protection of the ditch and huddled around Tomlinson, who said, "All right you guys, listen up. We have to check out what's on the other side of this valley to see if we draw any fire from the high ground; then we get out of here."

"Moeller, it's your lucky day, you get to take the point: We will give you cover from here and follow in 50-foot intervals," Tomlinson stated.

"Thanks, Sarge, you're all heart," Moeller said, spitting at the bank in front of him with tobacco juice dribbling off his chin.

"Okay, let's do it! The rest of you guys fan out and keep your eyes open. Go!" the sergeant ordered.

Moeller, my first cousin, knelt in the ditch, waiting for his buddies to take up their positions, studying the open ground he was about to cover. "No movement, nothing, maybe my luck will hold," he thought to himself. He glanced over at the sergeant, who was also surveying the expanse through his field glasses.

"Go. Keep low!" Tomlinson said.

The point man scrambled over the lip of the ditch and began zigzagging across the field, trying to make as small a target of himself as he possibly could.

He hadn't covered 50 feet when a muffled explosion sent the man sprawling. His helmet rolled to a stop 10 feet in front of him.

Sergeant Tomlinson gazed at the still figure. "He's dead, the field's mined." He was cut short by the staccato rattling of a machine gun as bullets ripped the turf before him. Crawling to a small bush at the edge of the ditch, he surveyed the valley and hill, trying to discover where the firing was coming from. "Could be a whole company out there. Keep down. Don't give our position away," he ordered his men.

Receiving no return fire, the enemy machine gun stopped firing, giving way to an eerie silence. The stillness was suddenly broken with a pleading, hardly discernible call: "Help me, I'm hit bad."

When the cries of the injured soldier were heard, the firing began again. Tomlinson crawled back to his vantage point at the lip of the ditch and looked out at the injured man. "There is no way we'll get him back. They're just waiting for us to try. They'll pick us off one at a time."

He crawled back to his men. "We'll wait until dark—it's only an hour or so away. We'll try to get him then, if he is still alive."

The moaning began again and Corporal Bex crawled over to the sergeant. "I'm going to get him. He'll freeze to death out there," Bex said.

"Negative, you don't stand a chance. Keep your head down and stay put," the sergeant told Bex.

The corporal knelt for a minute on the frozen ice. Then he crawled out of the ditch before anyone could stop him. He made it to within a few feet of the wounded man when a single shot rang out, stopping him in his tracks.

"Everyone stay put, you can't help Moeller. You're just dead meat out there," Tomlinson said. The men took their positions, trying to blot out the cries of the comrade, all except one.

Private First Class Richardson was kneeling on one knee, a prayer coming from tight lips: "Dear Lord, have mercy. If it be your will, then take both of us."

He reached for the crucifix tied around his neck, slipped it over his head, and held it in front of him as he climbed out of the ditch, leaving his weapon behind. Holding the cross over his heart, he walked toward the injured man, not bothering to run. Bullets tore up the ground around him, but none found their mark.

He reached down and picked up his buddy, who was barely conscious, and carried him back to the ditch.

Sergeant Tomlinson and Private Moeller were the only two men in the platoon alive at the end of the war. Although Moeller survived his injuries, he suffered the loss of one leg, blown off by the mine, and he lost a foot from frostbite. Moeller died of acute alcoholism 10 years later, never fully recovering from his ordeal.

Tomlinson carried the memories of that day with him and became a very religious man, but he was never able to answer the question that haunted him: were the two men shielded from certain death by that crucifix?

—Bill Kiene, Republic, Missouri
June 1995

Divine Retribution

I had this experience in May 1960 when I was 10 years of age. I quite remember it as if the occurrence were only a year old. It happened when my mother

Adzoa Asempah won a weekly lottery of 400 cedis and decided to collect her winnings at the district center where the lottery was staked. The town is called Vakpo, in the Kpandu district of Ghana.

After collecting her winnings, we joined our village-bound lorry and on reaching a point near my mother's farm we alighted and proceeded to her farm which lies about two miles away from our village.

In a few minutes' time, after we reached the farm, a man emerged from the bush. He came to stand in front of my mother and asked her if God could punish a wrongdoer immediately after the crime is committed or if the punishment would come later on.

My mother said she did not know. Then the man said that whether she knows or not, did she prefer to own the money which she collected from the lottery winnings and lose her life or to surrender the money to him and save her life?

My mother replied that if he was there because of that money he should take it. The man quickly took the money from my mother's bag and hurriedly went away. While he was going he insulted my mother saying over his shoulder, "You beast, you do not know how to spend money."

In a few minutes' time after the man had gone away we heard a male voice crying for help. At first we were afraid to go there but when the cry continued unabated for about 20 minutes we decided to go and see what was happening.

On reaching there we saw the man who took my mother's money firmly in the grip of a trap. When he saw us he cried loudly and said that now he had seen the existence of God and pleaded to my mother to forgive him and to call people to rescue him.

We hurriedly went to our village to inform the chief of the matter. He detailed people to accompany us to the scene. On arrival there we found the criminal still in the grip of the trap. He was rescued and when questioned he confirmed the report that we made to the chief of the village. He was then sent to the police station for interrogation and subsequently charged to appear before the law court. His name is Akpe Kojo, alias Guy Cemetery.

He was sentenced to nine months' imprisonment and when passing sentence on him the judge told him that since he had come to know the existence of God it would be better for him to reform after he had served his sentence in jail. The sum of 400 cedis was returned to my mother by the court.

—Joseph Anane, Kumasi, Ghana
July 1982

A Farewell With Whales

Mid-July, and the path lifted and twisted its way along the granite bluffs overlooking the softly-breathing evening sea. The sun was beginning its eastward descent behind the dark Nova Scotia spruce forests to the west. Its light, however, was still strong and had an almost golden clarity in the way it lit the far distant shores which marked the eastern arm of the approaches to Halifax harbor.

I kept my eyes on the ground, ready for a sudden twist in the narrow pathway, or for the unsteady rock anxious to shift in its unsteady setting. Only occasionally did I lift my head to look for the knot of people marking my destination. Soon enough, perhaps a mile from where I had left my car, there they were. About as ready as I was, I supposed, to commit the ashes of my oldest son, Keith, to the sea, to God, and to eternity. July 16, 1999, was not a day I had been looking forward to.

Keith's wife Cathy had chosen the spot. Later I was to learn that it held special meaning for the two of them. Some seven months ago, the Cessna 172 had crashed about 100 miles to the south, with Keith at the controls and his 19-year-old brother David with him in the right-hand seat. Now, at least, while the investigation into the crash was still dragging on, there would be some resolution for Cathy, a resolution beyond the funeral.

As for me, well, it was difficult to say.

I shook hands a little breathlessly with the small group gathered there, perhaps 30 feet above the sea. There was Cathy, of course, and her father and brother. The rest were Keith's friends, mostly familiar faces, with some tears in their eyes. They had come, like me, to say some sort of goodbye and, also like me, they were uncertain in the face of this event.

Cathy started things off, her back to the sea. Clouds far distant across the bay reflected tinges of rose even though dusk was still an hour away. Her voice catching, and with tears in her eyes, Cathy explained why we were there, what she hoped from this gathering of friends and kin, and how we might proceed over the next few minutes.

Then, as she spoke, a strange and almost magical thing began to happen.

Looking out beyond her, we could see another gathering on the smooth and gently rolling surface of the sea.

Whales—minkes by the look of them—and moving toward us with that fluid grace which is almost unique to this, the smallest of the rorquals. Two, then three—no, four—five! Their path seemed specific and direct until they were about 50 yards from the granite shore. Then, almost lazily, they began to patrol in large circular tracks, each whale seemingly independent of the others, but all of them coming back to that critical point directly opposite our small service.

They were there as many of us spoke in turn about our memories of Keith, and I spoke too, grieving both for him and for his younger brother David. They were there, too, as each of us scrambled down the face of the bluff to take a handful of my son's ashes and cast them into the sea. They were there, circling in a smooth and liquid silence and the sound of their breathing, like that of all minkes, was inaudible.

They were there as the last gray cloud of ash drifted away on a tender westerly breeze, and we all watched them, then looked at each other, and said nothing, perhaps afraid that speaking of their presence might break the spell that had brought the whales to us.

I had to leave ahead of the others, so I do not know how long the pod stayed off that promontory, watching, slipping under the surface, and then re-emerging with great soundless sighs. But I do know that one whale left the others to accompany me back along that mile or so of narrow track to where I had left my car.

At first, I thought the minke was simply following the arc of its own circular track as I had watched them all do during our simple headland service. But soon it became obvious that this particular whale was coming right along the shoreline, never ahead of me nor behind, but always parallel to my path whether I was 100 feet from the sea's edge or close enough to taste the salt of its presence.

Minkes can exceed 20 knots for significant periods of time, but this one just seemed to laze along, recognizing perhaps the limitations of a man over 60 moving at his own pace in rough terrain.

Whenever I looked, the whale was there, and I began to regret that I would soon be at the point where I would have to turn my back to the sea and climb the short slope to my car.

When that time came, I paused, and from the hill-top above I could hear excited voices: "Look, it's a whale!" There were others there, taking time to enjoy and admire the sea in this almost perfectly still evening. "What is it? Is that a whale?"

For a moment I felt like calling back, "Yes, and it's my whale!"

I did no such thing, of course. Instead, before turning up the hill, I waved. I waved goodbye, and then wiped my hands across my eyes. At my wave, the minke turned and headed out to sea. So I waved again and watched as this particular moment of magic faded back into a world and a life I could never know or understand.

"So long, buddy," I said, and I cried a little more as I climbed the hill.

—John H. Sansom, Halifax, Nova Scotia
July 2000

Beyond the Veil

One day in late November 1962, my father Fred Arnone, my uncles Salvatore and Edward Maugeri, and I were on a hunting trip in upstate New York. We arrived at the site at about 7:00 A.M. and decided to separate into two groups to better our chances of bagging a deer. The ground was covered with 10 to 12 inches of snow and more was coming down as we left the parking area. Uncle Sal and I went in a northeast direction while Dad and Uncle Eddie went northwest.

We spent more than an hour moving cautiously over streams, through thickets, and across a large field looking for an ideal post for the day's hunt. Crossing the field I noticed a tall stand of pines and thought it would be the perfect place to find deer. Approaching the pines, we were confronted by a thick wall of underbrush; penetrating it was difficult. Finally, entering the pines through a small opening, we were astounded by what we saw. The pine trees stood in perfectly straight rows in an area 500 yards long and 300 yards wide. Only about two inches of snow covered the ground in this area and at the far end the sun was shining. It was unbelievable.

Mystified, I turned back to look at our place of entry; there it was still snowing and the sky was heavily overcast. Then I started to run toward the sunny area with Uncle Sal behind me, shouting for me to stop, but I kept running until I reached the end of the pines. I groped through another wall of underbrush, this one green and flowering, and entered an area of about three to five acres of green grass, flowers, birds singing and squirrels chattering. The temperature was near 80 degrees. Impossible, I thought.

Uncle Sal had caught up with me. I said, "Sal, do you see what I see?"

Dumbfounded, he said, "Where the heck are we?"

We took off our heavy winter outer clothing and stretched out on a small hill to enjoy a mid-November summer's day. After about 45 minutes I suddenly realized that Dad and Eddie would never believe us so I told Uncle Sal we had better bring them here to show them. On our return trip to the car we were careful not to disturb our tracks leading in.

When we joined Dad and Uncle Eddie for lunch at the car, we told them what we had seen. Then the four of us followed our tracks to the pines and went through—but this time there was no sunshine at the other end. I ran ahead, thinking that we had left this place only an hour ago and now it had all changed. The others followed me through the underbrush and found me standing in awe. Our tracks leading to the small hill and the impressions of our bodies where we had lain showed that the snow was 12 inches deep.

What had happened? Did Sal and I have the same dream? Or did we step into another dimension? For many years thereafter I searched for that stand of pines but never found it again.

—Patrick F. Arnone, Monroe, New York
April 1982

Walk in the Woods

As an amateur hunter of the strange and supernatural in the late 1970s and early 1980s, I have many unusual happenings under my belt, about which I enjoy telling. My friend Gary was a true unbeliever, only listening to the stories out of friendship. One day in mid-1982 I decided to take him to a place in the mountains where something strange would happen to me almost every time I went there.

We drove into the mountains behind Sulton, Washington, and parked the car at the end of an old logging road I knew about. Once the car was locked we went for a walk. Before the walk really began we had to cross two water-filled ditches and a large fallen tree. It was 10:01 A.M. when we began our hike.

It was a warm day with a clear sky. Heat shimmers, like those seen on a long stretch of hot highway, were rising from the ground all around us, seemingly never more than 20 feet away.

We passed through a forest of old growth pine and fir trees, some of which were eight feet or more in diameter. We passed through a pristine meadow where several black-tailed deer were feeding. The deer watched us pass without alarm, and because of the velvet antlers carried by two of them, I vowed to remember this area.

Beyond the meadow, we crossed a new wood plank bridge, and then entered a clear-cut area (from logging). We then entered more old growth forest.

In this area of forest we found a brand new, royal blue, mid-1960s Ford Mustang, with a black vinyl convertible top and leather interior in mint condition. After a quick, envious look inside, we continued.

Shortly after the Mustang was out of sight, we crossed another new bridge of the same type as the first. Beyond this bridge we stopped to rest. I looked at my watch, disappointed that nothing had happened. It was 2:20 P.M. We had been walking for four straight hours without a break. Gary was as disappointed as I was.

The terrain had changed into brush and vine maple, and clouds were beginning to appear, which caused the heat shimmers to subside very quickly. We decided that we would start back after our rest. We'd brought nothing except a knife and compass with us and did not want to spend the night.

When we started back, I checked my watch—the time was 2:32 P.M. On the return walk, things started to get strange. The bridge which we'd passed over 20 minutes earlier was rotten and had collapsed, forcing us to get wet. Then we found the Mustang.

It was a total wreck—rusted, bullet holes, no paint, no top, and no interior. There was nothing made of any material except metal on the entire car. The terrain around us was still brush and remained so until we got to my car.

Both ways during the walk we followed a logging road. There were not offshoot roads anywhere along the road. However, we never found the old growth forests we'd walked through, or the meadow, or the logged area. It took us 11 minutes to walk the return trip to my car.

Following Gary's advice, even though I didn't want to, we left the area in a hurry. We got back to Seattle around 4 P.M. My watch said we'd been gone for eight hours, but my parents and Gary's job said we'd been gone for 32 hours. To the best of my knowledge there was no missing time during that day, and we did not spend the night.

Gary called me the day after we returned to tell me that he had missed a day at work and that he didn't know what I'd done, but he was not interested in any more trips to anywhere with me. I have seen him only once since that day, when he introduced me to his new son.

In June 1992, I decided to try to find this area again. Parking my car at the same spot, I went for a walk. I walked for almost three miles but never found the Mustang or any bridge or stream. After the first few yards or so, everything was logged off with new growth that was five to eight years old (a rough guess).

Was it time travel, dimension travel, or mutual insanity? Or am I missing a logical explanation?

—Scott Barber, Seattle, Washington
February 1994

PSYCHIC PETS & SPIRIT ANIMALS

True Stories from the Files of FATE Magazine

***FATE Magazine* Editorial Staff**

In spite of all our scientific knowledge about animals, important questions remain about the nature of animal intelligence. Now, a large body of personal testimony compels us to raise still deeper questions. Are some animals, like some people, psychic? If human beings survive death, do animals? Do bonds exist between people and animals that are beyond our ability to comprehend?

Psychic Pets & Spirit Animals is a varied collection from the past fifty years of the real-life experiences of ordinary people with creatures great and small. You will encounter psychic pets, ghost animals, animal omens, extraordinary human-animal bonds, pet survival after death, phantom protectors, and the weird creatures of cryptozoology. Dogs, cats, birds, horses, wolves, grizzly bears—even insects—are the heroes of shockingly true reports that illustrate just how little we know about the animals we think we know best.

The true stories in *Psychic Pets & Spirit Animals* suggest that animals are, in many ways, more like us than we think—and that they, too, can step into the strange and unknowable realm of the paranormal, where all things are possible.

1-56718-299-2, 272 pp., mass market
$4.99

STRANGE BUT TRUE

From the Files of FATE Magazine

edited by Corrine Kenner & Craig Miller

Have you had a mystical experience? You're not alone. For almost fifty years, FATE readers have been reporting their encounters with the strange and unknown. In this collection, you'll meet loved ones who return from beyond the grave . . . mysterious voices warning of danger . . . guardian angels . . . and miraculous healings by benevolent forces. Every report is a firsthand account, complete with full details and vivid descriptions:

- *"Suddenly, a vision appeared at the foot of my bed. It was a young woman, wearing a sad expression on her strangely familiar face . . ."*
- *"Running across the clearing from one thickly wooded area to the other was a thin, hunched creature, covered with light gray hair . . ."*
- *"As I got closer to the white light, I heard a loud and forceful voice say, 'No!' . . ."*
- *"At that moment I whooshed back into my body and sat up . . ."*

Whether you're a true believer or a die-hard skeptic, you'll find *Strange but True* a book you can't put down.

1-56718-298-4, 256 pp., 5 3/16 x 8
$9.95

TO ORDER, CALL 1-800-THE MOON

Prices subject to change without notice.

OUT OF TIME AND PLACE

Amazing Accounts that Challenge Our View of Human History

compiled and edited by Terry O'Neill from the files of *FATE Magazine*

"I held my hand out of the wagon window and caught four fat, brown little toads . . . I had heard of fish and frogs falling from the clouds, but I had never heard of a fall of toads . . ."

— "Does it Rain Toads?"

Explore fascinating mysteries of history, archaeology, and the paranormal with this collection of amazing reports published only in the pages of FATE magazine. The writers of these fascinating articles follow the footsteps of Indiana Jones, seeking the lost and trying to solve the mysteries of the oddly found. Thirty original articles from the best of FATE over the past forty years feature tales of lost cities, strange falls from the sky, extraordinary creatures, and misplaced artifacts that call into question our entire view of human history.

Despite studies by historians and scientists from many fields, these events and objects from out of time and place remain unexplained. Readers can't resist being enthralled by these mysteries and by the efforts to solve them.

1-56718-261-5, 272 pp., $5\frac{3}{16}$ x 8,
$9.95

TO ORDER, CALL 1-800-THE MOON

Prices subject to change without notice.